# COTTER ON INVESTING

# COTTER ON INVESTING

TAKING THE BULL OUT OF THE MARKETS—
PRACTICAL ADVICE AND TIPS FROM AN
EXPERIENCED INVESTOR

JOHN COTTER

Hh

HARRIMAN HOUSE LTD

3A Penns Road
Petersfield
Hampshire
GU32 2EW
GREAT BRITAIN

Tel: +44 (0)1730 233870
Fax: +44 (0)1730 233880
Email: enquiries@harriman-house.com
Website: www.harriman-house.com

First published in Great Britain in 2011

Copyright © John Cotter

The right of John Cotter to be identified as the Author has been asserted in accordance
with the Copyright, Design and Patents Act 1988.

ISBN: 978-0857190192

*British Library Cataloguing in Publication Data*
A CIP catalogue record for this book can be obtained from the British Library.

Set in Minion, Bebas Neue and FrutigerMW Cond.

Printed and bound in the UK by CPI Antony Rowe.

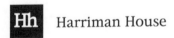 Harriman House

# CONTENTS

# DISCLAIMER

Nothing in this book should be taken as specific advice or as a specific recommendation to buy or sell a particular stock. Hopefully, however, much of what I have said will act as a catalyst to your investment thought processes.

Always remember that the value of shares can fall as well as rise and you can get back less than you invested.

During bad times in the market it may be necessary to remind yourself that shares can rise as well as fall. During 2008 I used to say this to myself as a daily mantra!

In the book I have used specific examples and prices to help demonstrate and bring to life the different principles and concepts involved. Obviously, the prices, ratios and charts were taken at the time of writing and will no longer be accurate, but are used to illustrate the principles involved.

At the time of writing, I own long-term investments in Medusa Mining, Tullow Oil, Communisis, Axis-Shield, Xstrata, BHP Billiton, Straight, Cookson Group and ASOS. Shares are also held on my behalf inside an employees' share scheme in Barclays Bank, but not in any other shares mentioned in this book.

# BIOGRAPHY

John has worked for the Barclays for 38 years, filling various senior management positions in the financial services industry. During the last 15 years he has worked for Barclays Stockbrokers, for whom he now fills the role of Vice President. He is a regular speaker on their behalf at client seminars and other professional gatherings and is renowned for his ability to demystify even the most complex of financial subjects.

John writes a regular column, *Cotter's Corner,* which is consistently one of the most popular sections on the Barclays Stockbrokers website. The articles aim to educate, inform and inspire investors of all levels, helping them to understand the ins and outs of investing and hopefully trade more profitably.

John is married with five children and has now returned to his native Merseyside to live.

# PREFACE

I have worked in the investment business for nearly 40 years and even now, after all this time, I often do not understand many of the investment reports and papers that are put in front of me written by experts. I am not questioning their knowledge or expertise, just their ability to communicate it in terms the average person can understand.

I was determined therefore to write a book on investing in shares that didn't confuse the average layman with technical jargon. A book that spoke about stock market investment the way I believe it is – a relatively straightforward subject that is best kept simple.

To make sure I pass my own simplicity test, when I use a phrase or word that I think the average person may not fully understand, I have included a simple explanation of it in a glossary at the end of the book.

This book, therefore, is written for people who want to make their own investment decisions in the stock market – a group of people we'll call *self-directed investors*.

The stock market of course can be a dangerous place and the risk involved can put people off the whole idea of investing in shares. It shouldn't. Successful investors are those who manage risk, not avoid it altogether. After all, a life without risk is a life without reward!

This book is not designed to be a comprehensive introduction to the topic of investing in shares. There are other books that do that already. Rather, I focus on a few key topics that I've found investors are most interested in.

I give my own opinions, not only on some of the different investment vehicles you can use, but also on the ways in which you can improve your performance as a self-directed investor, by using different selection and timing techniques. For me to promote an idea in this context it has to pass what I refer to as the

"3 Box Test": it has to be simple, it has to make sense and it has to work most of the time. If such an idea in my opinion ticks all three of these boxes, I have used it in this book. If it doesn't, I haven't.

If you do decide to take control of your own share portfolio I think you will find it not only financially beneficial, but also an enjoyable learning experience.

Good luck with your investing!

# CHAPTER 1:

## WHY BUY SHARES?

## Your financial future

I don't think that being financially self-sufficient is just a preferred option anymore, I believe it is essential. Gone are the days when Mr Average would work 40 years of his life for one company and retire with a pension equal to two-thirds of his final salary. The prospects for the state pension are equally dismal. Not only will the amount payable come under immense pressure, but the existing plans to defer the qualifying date to 66 from 65 will only be the start of a slippery slope.

The institutions that used to look after us can no longer be relied on to do so; whether this is your employer, the government or the NHS. For Mr and Mrs Average, who have aspirations of a quality life both while working and in retirement, the message is clear: if you don't provide it for yourself then no-one else is likely to do it for you.

And this is the way the world is going – we want to take control of our own lives in all sorts of ways. For instance, we are far less likely to buy a packaged holiday from a travel agent now than we used to be. Many more people not only want to take more control of their holidays but also their investments.

So, to get started, there are two big questions every potential investor should ask themselves:

1.    Should stock market investments play an important part in my life?

2.    Should I take responsibility for my own investment decisions?

I strongly believe that the answer to both questions is yes. Let me explain by addressing each point in turn. First, should you buy shares?

# Are shares a good investment?

## The long-term

How's this for a fact:

> If you invested £1000 in 1945 in the broad UK stock market, by the end
> of 2009 it would be worth almost £1.2million![1]

A problem is that not many people are patient enough to take a 65-year view!
However, I make no apologies for quoting such a long-term figure. Most
people's financial lives are divided into different stages. Very often they start
life as a *borrower*, then become a *saver*, then an *investor* and end up in
retirement as a *spender*. These financial stages are not mutually exclusive and
can and do co-exist at times. However, there always tends to be a dominant
theme at any one time that tends to progress in the above sequence. The
investment stage in the last few decades has been extended at the front end
by corporate share schemes, and at the back end by increased longevity. As
life expectancy continues to grow, 65 years could soon become the average
length of a person's investment life.

As impressive as this stock market performance is on its own, compared to
other types of assets it becomes even more so.

£1000 invested in the average cash deposit account over the same 65-year
period would be worth approximately £61,000 today.

£1000 invested in gilts would be worth around £51,000 today.[2]

Moving on to a comparison with the fourth asset class, property, the
performance of the stock market is equally impressive. It is more difficult to
compare property figures because of the regional nature of the market;
however, the Land Registry records show that in 1945 the average house price
in the UK was £1,400, while in 2010 it was £167,000. So, a £1000 investment
in the average house in the UK in 1945 would be worth £119,000 today.

So, we can see that the UK stock market over the 65-year period has produced
over 19 times more than the average deposit account, over 23 times more
than the average gilt, and around eight times the average UK property.

The following chart illustrates the long-term growth of the UK stock market:

---

[1] Barclays Equity and Gilt Study (BEGS) 2010
[2i] BEGS 2010

**Figure 1.1: FTSE All-Share Index, 1945-2011**

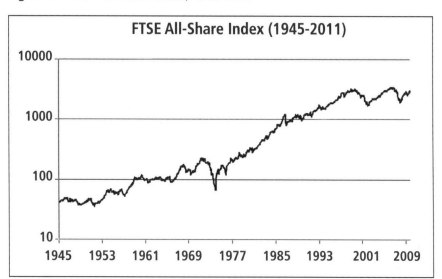

As can be seen in the preceding chart, the stock market has generally progressed upwards since 1945. But, this progress has not been a straight line; there have been set-backs, when the market has fallen.

*So, shares perform well over long periods – but what about over shorter time periods?*

## Shorter investing periods

The following table looks at a longer period (1899 to 2010) and compares the performance of shares against cash and gilts for every period since 1899 for a range of shorter-term investing periods:

| | Number of consecutive years | 2 | 3 | 4 | 5 | 10 | 18 |
|---|---|---|---|---|---|---|---|
| Cash | Out-perform cash | 72 | 75 | 78 | 79 | 92 | 92 |
| | Under-perform cash | 37 | 33 | 29 | 27 | 9 | 1 |
| | Total number of years | 109 | 108 | 107 | 106 | 101 | 93 |
| | Probability of equity out-performance(%) | 66 | 69 | 73 | 75 | 91 | 99 |
| Gilts | Out-perform gilts | 75 | 81 | 82 | 80 | 81 | 83 |
| | Under-perform gilts | 34 | 27 | 25 | 26 | 20 | 10 |
| | Total number of years | 109 | 108 | 107 | 106 | 101 | 93 |
| | Probability of equity out-performance(%) | 69 | 75 | 77 | 75 | 80 | 89 |

Source: Barclays Capital

For example, let's look at the second column of data, headed '3'. Since 1899, there have been 108 three-year consecutive periods (1899-1902, 1900-1903, 1901-1904 etc.). The table shows that an investment in shares for 75 of those 3-year periods would have out-performed cash. In other words, based on past performance, if you're looking to invest over a three-year period, there's a 69% probability that shares will out-perform cash. For the same three-year period, shares have out-performed gilts for 81 of the 108 periods, suggesting a probability for equity out-performance for any three-year period of 75%.

So, even for short investing periods, such as two or three years, based on history, equities have out-performed cash and gilts.

And as the investing period gets longer, the probability of equities out-performing cash and gilts increases.

This does not mean that cash and gilts have no part to play in your investment plan – we will see later they often do. What it does mean, however, is that shares should play a major part of any investment portfolio.

"As the investing period gets longer, the probability of equities out-performing cash and gilts increases."

The financial case for investment in the stock market, as far as I'm concerned, is an open and shut one.

So, you're convinced by the argument for investing in shares: should you let a professional look after your money for you or do it yourself?

# Do you trust yourself or a professional?

There are five points I'd like to make here:

## 1. Professionals aren't very good at investing

Many professional managers simply do not do a good job. The majority of actively managed funds under-perform the index they are seeking to out-perform.

## 2. Professional costs are high

The cost of professional management is significant, especially as the investment period grows. These can average between 2%-3% per annum.

These create major headwinds to overcome if long-term, out-performance of the market is to be achieved.

It is hardly surprising that 80% of actively managed funds fail to beat their benchmark as quite clearly the costs mean that they would have to consistently over-perform by 2%-3% per annum simply to cover the costs and match it.

In the long-term this becomes a huge factor. For example, if you invested £100,000 over a 25-year period and achieved a 7% annual return but paid annual charges of 3%, the overall return would be approximately £266,000. If the annual charges were limited to 1%, the return would be £440,000. If no charges were deducted, the return would amount to £525,000!

Let's put these figures in a table to really highlight them:

| Annual charge | Value of £100,000 invested |
|---------------|----------------------------|
| 3% | £266,000 |
| 1% | £440,000 |
| 0% | £525,000 |

The figures speak for themselves. Costs matter!

## 3. Small is beautiful

So, professional fund managers are not good at investing and are costly, but can you do better yourself? Well, investing in simple, cheap tracker funds (e.g. ETFs – more on these later) means you will out-perform the majority of professional fund managers for a start.

But there can actually be an advantage in being small. You can gain access to corners of the market that are, effectively, closed to the average managed fund due to their size. I have spoken to many professional managers who accept that a particular stock may be priced to offer value, but don't take advantage of the situation because the amount of the stock they could purchase would be totally insignificant compared to the value of their fund.

The famous investor, Jim Slater, when speaking about the merits of small companies, said:

> "Elephants don't gallop, but fleas can jump to over two hundred times their own height."

I believe that small can also be good when it comes to investors as well as companies!

## 4. Invest in what you know

Peter Lynch, the American investor, is convinced that the average investor can out-perform the professional fund manager. He popularised the concept of "Invest in what you know", which referred to the opportunity we all have in our daily lives to spot investment opportunities long before they are identified by fund managers looking at reports and figures.

He speaks about some of the best investments he has made first coming to his notice when he was driving around with his family or shopping at a local mall.

I believed in this concept long before I even heard of Peter Lynch and I have had the same experience. In a later chapter, I will go into some specific examples that should bring this concept as alive for you as it is for me.

## 5. Investing yourself is rewarding in many different ways

But there is more to all this than just money. Hopefully, as I have found myself, you will discover it can be fun, interesting and immensely satisfying to invest personally in the stock market. It also helps you to stay humble; on occasions you can be intellectually correct but still lose money!

I agree that if you constantly lose out in your stock market ventures it is highly doubtful you will stick around to appreciate these finer points. However, most of the long-term self-directed investors I know, who follow sensible rules, make money.

So, you've made the decision to invest yourself, but how practical is this?

# Is it feasible to invest yourself?

The good news is that it has never been easier to manage your own investments. In this area, as in many others, the internet has changed things dramatically.

On websites today there is a wealth of information and research available to make investment selection and self-management far easier than ever before. But it's not just about being a more informed investor. The websites also provide investors with many tools that make management and investment choice much easier and quicker. You can rank companies by dividend yield, earnings growth, PEGs – and much more. Stock filters that carry out searches for you for stocks that match whatever criteria that you want are understandably popular and extremely useful (don't worry if you don't understand all these terms, most will be covered later in the book).

The online platforms also allow you to deal at a fraction of the cost that used to apply. Dealing from £5 to £15 flat rates are now common. On the subject of dealing, it has to be said that the use of limits, stops and trailing stop orders make dealing much more effective and reduce risk. I will devote a separate chapter to this whole subject. These platforms make effective self-management of your investments a relatively straightforward task.

In summary investing in the stock market over the long term can have a very beneficial effect on your wealth! Controlling the investments yourself and making your own decisions has never been easier and is interesting and fun. In the long-term, annual management charges made by professionals make it entirely possible for the average layman to outperform them.

Why don't you give it a try? If you have doubts, why not split your investments and measure your performance against the professionals. You may be surprised just how good you are!

# CHAPTER 2:

## A COMMON SENSE
## APPROACH TO INVESTING

## The application of common sense

As Warren Buffett once pointed out, investment is not a subject in which the person with the highest IQ will do best. I for one take great comfort in this view. I have always thought that investment is a relatively straightforward subject that is best kept simple.

It constantly amazes me how many people who are successful in their business lives seem to struggle when it comes to investing money. They should analyse why they have been successful in their own fields. Very few will have been technical experts. Most will have had a general interest in the area of the market concerned and would have adopted what many would describe as a common sense approach.

It seems to me many forget these principles when they enter the world of investment or decide, wrongly, to delegate the management of their money to people who are less able than they are.

### Back to basics

Let's go back to the very basics before we draw up some simple guidelines that hopefully will help.

When you buy shares in a company you become one of the owners of that business. The extent of your ownership is dictated by the number of shares you own compared to the total number in issue. The total value of a quoted company is referred to as its *market capitalisation* (often abbreviated to market cap), and this is calculated by multiplying the total number of shares by the current share price.

## What's in it for you?

As the part owner of the business you are entitled to two financial benefits:

1.  A share of the **current capital value of the business** represented by the current share price.

2.  A share of the **annual profits**. A proportion of these is often paid out each year as an income and is referred to as a dividend.

This being the case, you should ask yourself what type of business you would like to own. If you were buying the entire business you would undoubtedly think very carefully about this. You should do the same when it comes to buying shares.

## Invest in what you know

Warren Buffett talks of this as the investor's *circle of confidence*. It's obvious, and only common sense, that the investor should focus on areas or sectors that interest them and they know best. At the very least the investor should appreciate what a company does and how it makes money. Often when I speak to investors about their shareholdings they have no idea what a company they own actually does!

The American investor, Peter Lynch, had a similar idea when he recommended investors to *invest in what you know*. He believes that the individual investor has an advantage over the professional fund manager because he believes they have more of a normal life than fund managers stuck in Wall Street. He records the fact that he has found some of his best investments when he was just going about his normal life.

I agree with Lynch's thinking. If you keep your eyes open and your brain turned on when just living your life, you can spot great stock market opportunities – long before the figures become visible even to the most perceptive of stock market professionals.

## Examples

Let me give you a few personal examples that illustrate that good investments are not only found in the *Financial Times* or broker's reports:

## 1. ASOS [ASC]

The first involves an old favourite of mine and goes back to April 2005. I came in from work and found my three young teenage daughters gathered around a laptop. I asked what was so interesting and they replied ASOS! I asked them a few questions about the company, more out of politeness than real interest.

I thought no more about this until the next morning when I was waiting to do a training presentation in Glasgow to a largely young female audience of new recruits. While waiting for a few latecomers, and more to break the awkward silence than for any other reason, I asked had anyone heard of ASOS. The majority of the girls put their hands up and spoke in positive terms, as my daughters had the night before, about the company's website, the style of clothes and the prices.

After the session I checked the company out on the website and I liked a number of things about it. It also had a low PEG [explained in a later chapter], which helped me make the decision to buy some shares for 51p on 19 April 2005. I then bought some more at 77p in November of that year, and more in July 2007 for £1.23. Subsequently, on three separate occasions I sold part of my holding to take profits, but I still hold some shares – currently priced at over £18.

There is no doubt in my mind if it wasn't for seeing my three daughters huddled around the laptop, and the reaction I got to my questions the following day in Glasgow, I would never have even heard of the company until the share price was at least eight times higher than the level at which I first bought at.

## 2. easyJet [EZJ]

Another example of spotting investment opportunities in everyday life would be easyJet.

In 2008 I had cause to fly with them for pleasure and business about a dozen times. I had only used them a few times before so my regular use in this year was sheer chance. Although not every aspect of the service was a joy (Speedy Boarders!), overall it was a very positive experience and attractively priced. I noticed that the flights had very few empty seats, in-flight food was purchased at every row and staff on board seemed to appreciate that customers have a choice (not always the case!) This made me think it was a business in which I would be happy to be a co-owner.

I bought shares in December 2008 at £2.52 and took profits from half of the holding just one year later at £4.60. Although the share price has been a little erratic since (due to ash clouds, snowed-in airports etc.), it still stands a fair way above my purchase price.

### 3. Straight [STT]

The final example focuses on wheelie bins!

I noticed that the number of different bins we had at home had increased from one to three. I then stayed with a friend in Motherwell and noticed they had four, all in different colours! I travel a lot for business and driving around, keeping my eyes open, it appeared that wheelie bins seemed to be growing on every street corner faster than a triffid in a compost heap! It wasn't just the bins, but the whole concept of recycling that caught my imagination. I made some enquiries and discovered that Straight was a company with a significant stake in the wheelie bin market and was growing both by acquisition and organically.

I bought shares in the company at 67p in June 2009 and today they are priced at 115p (hopefully with more growth to come as I still own them).

## The lessons

All three of the above examples are investments I originally discovered when I was just living my normal daily life. Obviously, I researched them properly after they had come to my attention, but the fact is they only came to my notice originally when I was chatting to my daughters, flying about or just driving around my local neighbourhood. It pays to keep your investment brain switched on even when you are away from your laptop!

# Keeping it simple

Another point I want to make, which in a way is closely connected in conceptual terms to Buffett's "circle of confidence" and Lynch's "investing in what you know", is the idea of focusing on simplicity when you select the companies you invest in.

The point I want to make here is that some businesses are a lot easier to understand than others. I suggest you make things easier for yourself by vetting out the difficult investment opportunities early in the selection process. The more straightforward the business of a company, the better.

Look again at the three example investments I gave above; they were involved in selling clothes, transport, and making wheelie bins. None of that is very sexy or complicated – just simple, solid businesses.

The greater the clarity in a company's operations and how and where it makes money, the more attractive as an investment proposition it becomes. I find that opaque is not a good style for a company to adopt for its business plan if it wants me as a co-owner. Nor for the great Warren Buffett, who famously said:

*"never invest in a business you cannot understand."*

Nevertheless, some companies seem to go out of their way to muddy the waters. Very often this happens when a company grows by means of multiple acquisitions over a short period. I think you need to be very careful when this happens, as it becomes almost impossible to make comparisons or judgements on a like-for-like basis. They seem to never stand still long enough to do so.

Let me give you an example of a company that I believe achieves the clarity that I seek.

Medusa Mining [MML] is a high-grade, low-cost gold producer based in the Philippines. It is actually one of the world's cheapest gold producers as it currently produces it at a cost of less than US$190 per ounce. It sells it for more than US$1300. How is that for a simple business case?

Why would you not want to be the co-owner of a business that digs something out of the ground and sells it on for 650% more than it costs to dig it up?

I believe companies with business cases as straightforward as this are ones to put on your investment shortlist. Make life easier for yourself by taking the complicated ones off!

# CHAPTER 3:
## THE PE RATIO

Over the next couple of chapters I will look at what I regard as the two most important methods of evaluating a share: the PE and the PEG ratios. I will start with the Price Earnings ratio (PE), one of the oldest and most widely used measurements.

## What is it used for?

The PE measures the value placed on a share by the market–this value is sometimes referred to as a share's *rating*.

It has two main applications as a measure of relative value to see whether a share is cheap or expensive:

1.  **For individual stocks**
    It can be used to compare the relative value of the current price of one share against another share, or against an index or sector.

2.  **For overall market levels**
    It can be used as a means to evaluate how cheap or expensive a whole market, or a sector, is compared to their long-term average or to other markets or sectors.

## Why is it important?

The relationship between the value of a company and its level of profits is obviously a very important one. The correlation between share price growth and earnings per share growth is positive and in the long-term very close. Clearly, as the profits of a company rise the price of its shares will ultimately follow – the problem for investors is the exact timing of the share price response to rising profits.

If we can forecast the profits of a company (and this is often possible) and we understand the relationship between a company's profit growth and share price growth then this provides a possible solution to forecasting future share prices.

## Calculating the PE

The PE ratio basically compares the market value of a company with its profits.

To calculate the PE we use the share price to represent the market capitalisation and earnings per share (EPS) to represent profits. The formula for the PE ratio is:

$$\text{PE ratio} = \frac{\text{share price}}{\text{earnings per share}}$$

For example, if a company's share price is 36p and its earnings per share are 4p, its PE ratio is nine (sometimes expressed as "9x" – meaning "nine times").

If a company does not have earnings (i.e. they are making a loss) then a PE can not be calculated.

One way of looking at the PE ratio is as representing the number of years required for the earnings per share to cover the share price.

Let's look at two companies:

| | Company A | Company B |
|---|---|---|
| Share price(p) | 100 | 100 |
| Earnings per share(p) | 20 | 50 |
| PE | 5 | 2 |

- Company A has a share price of 100p and EPS of 20p; it therefore has a PE of 5 (100/20); it would take *5 years* for the earnings to cover the price paid for the share.

- Company B has a share price of 100p and EPS of 50p; it therefore has a PE of 2 (100/50); it would take *2 years* for the earnings to cover the price paid for the share.

All things being equal (which, admittedly, they rarely are in investing) an investor would prefer to buy company B rather than company A because the earnings will pay for the price paid in just two (instead of five) years.

One way to think of this is as an investor buying the whole company. In the case of company A, it will take five years for the company's earnings to repay the price paid to buy the company, But for company B it will only take two years. Which company would you prefer to buy?

In this context, company B is called *cheaper* than company A because its PE ratio is lower.

Unfortunately, nothing in life is as simple as you would like it to be and few things are as difficult as keeping things simple. Let's first of all see how this position becomes more confused before hopefully I reach a simple and logical conclusion that will help guide your future use of the PE.

## Different types of PE

When calculating PE ratios in real life, it is easy to find a company's share price, but what figure should we use for EPS? For example, should we use the company's earnings from last year or its forecast earnings for this year? Because of the different values of EPS that can be used, there are three basic types of PE ratio. All are based on the current price, but one is based on previous earnings, one is based on forecast earnings and one is based on average earnings.

1.  **Trailing PE:** This is based on the actual earnings for the previous 12 months and is sometimes referred to as the *historic PE*.

2.  **Cyclically adjusted PE:** This uses earnings averaged over periods as long as ten years; often referred to by its acronym *CAPE*.

3.  **Forward PE:** This is based on the forecast earnings for the coming 12 months and is often referred to as the *forecast PE*.

The following table gives some sample real-life data for trailing and forecast PEs:

| Company | Share price | Trailing EPS | Trailing PE | Forecast EPS | Forecast PE |
|---|---|---|---|---|---|
| ARM Holdings | 545 | 6.44 | 84.6 | 9.96 | 54.7 |
| Aviva | 434 | 50.40 | 8.6 | 64.55 | 6.7 |
| Severn Trent | 1441 | 130.64 | 11.0 | 92.56 | 15.6 |
| Tesco | 388.5 | 26.29 | 14.8 | 32.72 | 11.9 |

For example, in the previous 12 months Tesco had an earnings per share of 26.29p, and at the time of writing its share was 388.5p; therefore its trailing PE was 14.8 (388.5/26.29). However, for the coming 12 months Tesco has a forecast EPS of 32.72p, which gives it a forecast PE of 11.9 (388.5/32.75).

*So which is best?*

Different people have different views. The trailing PE is one that is quoted most often in the financial press. The main advantage of this method is that you are dealing with facts, not forecasts. The CAPE has had, and still has, its followers; some notable ones include Benjamin Graham and Robert Shiller. The advantage of the CAPE is that it eradicates the possibility of the ratio being distorted by one year's figures. A moving average over a minimum of five years should mean that the sample period includes at least one complete economic cycle. And this measure is supported by the logic that company and index ratings will in time revert to their mean.

While both of the preceding have merit and cannot be dismissed lightly, my first point of reference will always be the one year forward PE.

Although the trailing PE is based on verified figures, you don't drive a car by looking in your rear view mirror, therefore I prefer this year's forecasts to last year's facts. The same comment applies to the CAPE but even more so. There is no doubt the CAPE will eradicate the chance of one set of figures giving a misleading reading, and although CAPE may be ideal for long-term financial studies, I cannot accept that earnings figures that could stretch back over a decade ago should play a part in tomorrow's investment decision. The market itself is a forward looking animal. It's a barometer, not a thermometer, and will always discount ahead. It therefore makes sense to use a measure that does the same.

**"I prefer this year's forecasts to last year's facts."**

## Interpretation of the PE

As mentioned above, the PE is a measure of the value placed on a company by the market. If investors like a company they will buy the shares, which will drive the share price up, which will result in a higher PE. This is a simple function of the calculation of the PE. Remember, the formula is:

$$\text{PE ratio} = \frac{\text{share price}}{\text{earnings per share}}$$

If the earnings per share stay the same but the share price increases, this results in a higher calculated PE.

Conversely, if investors dislike a company they will sell the shares, which will drive the share price down, which will result in a lower PE.

Companies with high PEs are often referred to as being *highly rated* by the market, while companies with low PEs are often referred to as being *lowly rated* by the market.

*But the big question is: what level is considered high (or low) for a PE? For example, is a PE of 20x considered high?*

There is no short answer to that question. Different people interpret the PE differently.

For example, growth investors may regard a PE of 30x as not unreasonable if a company is expected to grow strongly. Whereas a value investor (like Warren Buffett) prefer companies with low PEs. It is not surprising that Buffett never invests in technology companies (that often have high PEs).

Personally, I align myself with Buffett and prefers companies with low PEs. A low PE shows that the stock is cheap relative to its earnings. We know that price and earnings are inextricably linked, which makes the low PE stock a safer proposition with a lower downside risk.

## Using the PE to compare stocks

The absolute level of a share price tells us little about a company. Knowing that AstraZeneca has a share price of £28.74 and GlaxoSmithKline has a share price of £11.70 tells us nothing about the absolute or relative merits of these two companies. But comparing their PEs can be useful. In this case, AstraZeneca has a forward PE of 7.1x, while GlaxoSmithKline has a forward PE of 9x. This tells us that the market places a higher rating on GlaxoSmithKline than AstraZeneca. So, while its share price may be nominally cheaper, GlaxoSmithKline shares are regarded as more expensive than those of AstraZeneca.

The job of the investor is to consider whether the market has got it right. If an investor believes that the prospects for AstraZeneca are as good (or even better) than GlaxoSmithKline, then he would regard AstraZeneca as currently being good value relative to GlaxoSmithKline.

## Examples

Let me demonstrate how I use the PE to assess stocks.

The following table lists some stocks and their forecast PEs. For comparison, the market as a whole had a PE of 13.5.

| Company | Forecast PE |
|---|---|
| ASOS [ASC] | 70 |
| Dominos Pizza [DOM] | 33 |
| Aggreko [AGK] | 19 |
| GlaxoSmithKline [GSK] | 9 |
| Xstrata [XTA] | 9 |

The forecast PE shows that online clothes retailer **ASOS** is very expensive now after a period when it defied the recession with a share price rise of about 1500% over five years. After share price growth at this rate I suppose you would expect it to be expensive; and the PE shows it to be over five times more expensive than the average share. It may still be a quality company but without doubt you are now paying a high price for that quality.

Maybe more people like pizzas than I think, but the current PE rating on **Dominos** looks very expensive to me.

**Aggreko** is a global supplier of mobile power and has supplied events such as the football World Cup and the Olympics. It has been one of the stars of the FTSE in recent times with its PE increasing from nine three years ago to 20 at the time of writing. In other words, it has moved from a cheap share to a relatively expensive one. It is a company that I still like, but its present rating is a little high, which makes me think the stock price will, at least, pause for breath before resuming its growth.

The PE on **Glaxo** appears too low. It has moved from a growth stock to a value one with a PE of less than ten and a dividend of more than 5%. Have the heydays of the big pharmaceutical come to an end? Obviously, judging by its PE a lot of investors think so. It's true that fewer new drugs will come to the market in the future; and at the same time more of the old ones will lose their patent protection and face competition from cheaper generic versions. In addition, potential litigation costs are rising. Obviously, different views abound – after all, that's what makes a market in the first place. But I believe that this share is now too cheap. The present PE ratio would indicate to me that this company would justify inclusion in a portfolio as a lower-risk, high-dividend player. Although the growth potential is less than many shares, so is the downside. Successful stock investment is about investing in shares where the risk-reward ratio is skewed in your favour.

Finally, **Xstrata** [XTA] looks cheap with a PE of nine. Will growth in China and emerging markets continue to support the price of commodities? Obviously, this rating suggests that many think it will falter. However, this PE looks too cheap. In fact, many of the miners do. BHP Billiton [BLT] has a similar rating of ten which may suggest much of the mining sector is undervalued at the present time.

Obviously, the above views are purely personal and they have a limited shelf life. However, hopefully this quick overview demonstrates that when it comes to assessing individual shares PE ratios have a part to play.

In isolation they do not provide the whole picture, but they do provide a few pieces of the jigsaw. They provide a background against which the share and its current price can be assessed. They tell you whether the stock is cheap or expensive and once this is established you are able to make other value judgements. Used in this way, they can simply help you make more informed investment decisions.

## Using the PE to compare companies in different sectors

Some people feel when making stock comparisons the PE is only useful when you compare stocks within the same sector. Although I understand the logic here, I don't agree with it. Some sectors offer the promise of growth more than others (e.g. bio-techs) and this will be reflected overall in higher PEs. However, this simply means that the sector is more expensive. Investing within it inevitably means there is more downside risk as there is greater scope for disappointment. Although you should take into account the average ratings in each sector when making investment decisions, I believe cross sector comparisons using PEs are still valid and act as a useful reminder of the real price we are paying for a share.

## Market comparisons

I think the greatest strength of the PE is as a measure of the overall market. For example, the UK market has a long-term average PE of 15, while the world market has a long-term average PE of 16. These can be used as a guide to current value, and help determine the amount of money that should be invested in the different asset classes. When it comes to geographical diversification it can also inform choice. My view is simple: the lower the PE, the cheaper the market and the greater the value on offer.

The following table lists the trailing and forward PEs of the World and UK markets as at end 2010:

|  | UK | World |
|---|---|---|
| PE (2010) | 12.0 | 14.6 |
| PE (2011) | 10.6 | 12.7 |
| Long-term average | 15.0 | 16 |

Source: Factset MSCI Barclays wealth strategy

As these figures for the equity markets are below the long-term averages it would indicate to me that equities at present offer good value and therefore it is an asset class in which the investor should be overweight. This position is also supported by the following chart:

**Figure 3.1: PE of the MSCI world Index**

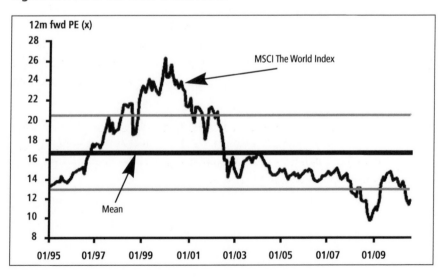

The chart shows that using the 1 year forward PEs as your guide, the world markets have been significantly undervalued

"The lower the PE, the cheaper the market and the greater the value on offer."

throughout 2009 and 2010 as the market PEs have been significantly below the long-term average (shown on the chart at just above 16).

I find the PE a better guide to value in the general markets than it is for individual shares.

It also helps to inform the timing of investment. There is plenty of historical evidence that shows the market PE is inversely correlated with subsequent stock market returns. In plain English this means that purchases made when market PEs have been below the long-term average (as they are now) have made more money in subsequent years than purchases made in years when the PE was relatively high.

"I find the PE a better guide to value in the general markets than it is for individual shares."

## The Rule of 20

This is a good place to mention what is known as *The Rule of 20*. This is an equity market valuation method that refines the use of the PE as a guide to value in the overall market. The rule works on the premise that fair value in the equity markets exists when the aggregate of the market PE and the current rate of inflation is 20. If the sum comes to less than 20, the rule suggests the market will rise. Over 20, and the rule indicates the market will fall. The more extreme the figure, either on the low or high side, the more certain the indication. In essence, the rule is a simplified dynamic asset allocation technique.

It's just a rule of thumb, but one which certainly passes my "3 Box Test" (referred to in the preface to this book). Over the years it has proved a very useful guideline that has helped me to decide whether to increase or decrease the current level of my equity investment.

# Conclusion

In summary, I believe the PE is a much better guide to value of the overall market than it is for individual shares. In fact, I would regard the one year forecast PE to be by far the best guide of value when it comes to general market levels.

With regard to individual shares, it is useful but certainly not the complete answer. In the following chapter we will look at what I believe is a better guide for share prices: the PEG.

---

Note: a table of PE values for the FTSE100 companies can be found in the appendix.

---

# CHAPTER 4:

## THE MIGHTY PEG

There are many methods you can use to pick a share, and everyone will have their own preferences. Some will seek out high dividends, some will follow the news, others read up on the broker's recommendations and many study the charts (mostly price, not astrological!). While all of these and other selection techniques have merit, when it comes to stock selection I believe the PEG is the king!

## What is the PEG?

In the previous chapter we looked at the PE ratio. We saw that while it was a useful measure, it does have limitations. For example, if company A has a PE of 12x and company B has a PE of 10x, then we can say that company A is *more expensive* (or has a *higher rating*) than company B. But that is all. The PE cannot tell us whether company A actually deserves its higher PE because its earnings are forecast to grow faster than those of company B. This is where the PEG comes in.

The PEG adds the factor of the forecast earnings growth to the PE calculation.

The formula to calculate the PEG is:

$$PEG = \frac{PE\ ratio}{forecast\ earnings\ growth}$$

The PEG acronym stands for *price earnings growth*, and its great strength is that it combines in one measure three key elements that investors need to assess a stock: price, earnings, and forecast earnings.

### The value of the PEG

In the long run, successful share investors are those who invest in companies whose shares are priced cheaply in relation to their current and future earnings. The PEG is a simple value measure that will enable you to find such shares and one which cuts across all normal market sectors and borders. It

> "The PE will highlight shares that are cheap, while the PEG will highlight shares that are undervalued."

therefore provides you with a method of comparing not only similar companies (i.e. in the same sector), but all companies.

Successful investors should be looking to factor in future growth into his or her calculations, and this is what the PEG will do. In essence, therefore, the PE will highlight shares that are cheap, while the PEG will highlight shares that are undervalued. There is a big difference.

## The GARP theory

The legendary Jim Slater popularised the PEG ratio, but it was Peter Lynch who introduced the GARP (Growth At a Reasonable Price ) theory – the idea underlying the PEG. In his book *One Up on Wall Street* he wrote:

> "The PE ratio of any company that is fairly priced will equal its growth rate."

To me this makes perfect sense, and as a rule of thumb it is something I always bear in mind when evaluating possible share purchases.

The GARP theory suggests that if a company's share price is at its fair value then it will have a PEG of one. A PEG of less than one would indicate that the shares are undervalued; a PEG of over one that the shares are overvalued.

I love simple ideas that make sense and work most of the time. The GARP theory certainly ticks all three boxes for me!

# Using the PEG

As I have already said I find one of the great benefits of using the PEG ratio is that it provides a means to make a value comparison on very different companies: those in different situations and different sectors.

For example, a company that is boring and cheap with a PE of eight and forecast growth of 8% has a PEG of one (8/8). Whereas a company that may be exciting but expensive with a PE of 30 and forecast growth of 30% also has a PEG of one. Just being cheaper (i.e. having a lower PE) does not necessarily make the first company a better buy.

I suggest that you let the PEG determine which stocks are the better value. The lower the PEG, the better the value.

## Example

As an aid to stock selection, in most situations I find the PEG has no equal and the more I have used it the better investor I have become. I find it does not just inform my selections but can also help time my exits.

Take ASOS [ASC], a share I have written about before as an example. In the winter 2007 edition of Smart Investor, the Barclays Stockbrokers client magazine, I made this one of my two shares to follow. One of the main reasons for this was the PEG ratio, which at the time was 0.8 (when the share price was 110p). As the price quadrupled, the PEG also improved from 0.8 to 0.6. The PEG was saying that ASOS was a better buy at 500p than it had been at 110p!

*How is that possible?*

Well, simply because the forecast earnings growth had increased more than the price.

As you can see from the following chart, the share price in 2008 and 2009 rose steadily; but this price rise was outpaced by the forecast earnings growth as evidenced by the falling PEG. Moving into 2010, the share price rose at a faster pace and this accelerated trend eventually brought the falling PEG to a halt. When the share price rose almost vertically, the PEG also eventually began to rise.

**Figure 4.1: ASOS**

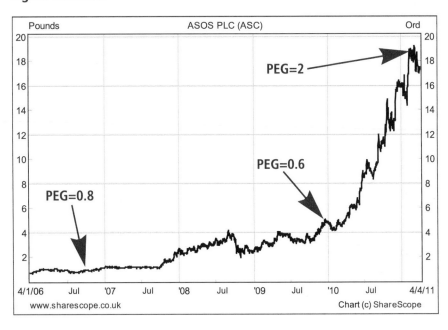

35

The share price eventually rose to over £18. For the investor, a PEG of over 2 was saying: time to think about taking some profits. ASOS was, and is still, a good company, but at that price the PEG was saying it was no longer undervalued. Used in this way, a PEG therefore does not just inform selection but can also time your exits or partial withdrawals from a stock.

The whole balance between price, current earnings and earnings growth can be a delicate one and, of course, you are dealing with a dynamic situation. It's possible that an increase in future earnings could once again reverse the rise in the PEG. However, as a simple rule of thumb, using the PEG in this manner to time stock entrances and exits works for me.

## Trading and the PEG

If you were trend trading this share, the position in my opinion would be different. Although the low PEG may have played a part in selection of the trade, the key point of focus for a trader is momentum. Although the rising PEG ratio may put the trend trader on alert to exit, he should stick with the trade while the positive momentum remains. Therefore, for the trader, the 30-day and 90-day moving averages should be the method used to time the exit [I will go into this in some more detail in a later chapter].

It may seem strange to some that the method and timing of the exit may be different for the trader and investor. After all, it is the same share owned at the same time. However, as the legendary Benjamin Graham once said when discussing speculation:

> "It is perfectly proper to take speculative factors into account, which are different from investment factors."

There is no bigger factor for the trader to take into account than short-term momentum, so the trader should stay with the share until this reverses or at least subsides.

# PEG limitations

Like everything in life the PEG has its limitations:

1.  The PEG can not be calculated for companies that have no earnings growth or are not making a profit at all. Although there is always a place for the "jam tomorrow" investments in a portfolio, perhaps this is a reminder to us that the number of such companies in a portfolio should be kept to a minimum.

2.  The PEG tends to under-rate mature companies with high stable profits that you may find attractive for different reasons (such as a high dividend).

3.  If you are using the one-year forecast PEG (which is the one I would recommend) you do have to remember it is a forecast and forecasts are not always accurate.

4.  When calculating the PEG you should factor into your decision-making process the size of the company. For example, it may be easier to forecast earnings growth for a larger, established company with earnings around £100m than it is for an upstart with earnings under £1m. The larger the company and the profit the more robust and reliable the forecasts tend to be.

# Where to find PEG data

You will find the PEG is one of the most common measures and is widely quoted.

For example, they are on the Barclays Stockbroker website on the summary page for each company, and also under the financial tab (see the following screenshot):

## Figure 4.2: screenshot of Barclays Stockbroker web page

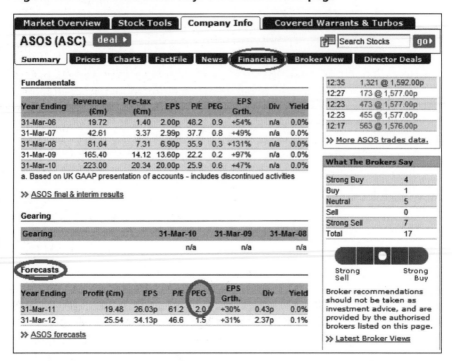

The stock filters on websites can also help you use the PEG to its full potential. The best filter on the Barclays Stockbroker website is found under the "stock selector" in the stock tools section. Go to the "build your own" section then to the full screener option. Under this you have scores of different options you can select to use in conjunction with each other.

The one I frequently use is under the sub heading "valuation ratios": the "next year forecast PEG". I would follow Peter Lynch's advice; in the minimum box insert 0.0 and in the maximum 0.9. According to the GARP theory, the shares it will identify will represent the most undervalued growth stocks on the London markets. This is a good shortlist to start with, and if you want to make it shorter just make the criteria stricter.

Along with the preceeding PEG requirements, I often insert a minimum forecast dividend of 3% with minimum cover of two. I think the combination of the potential growth, highlighted by the PEG, and the relatively high forecast income make an interesting cocktail...try mixing one yourself!

> Note: a table of PEG values at the time of writing for the FTSE100 companies can be found in the appendix.

# CHAPTER 5:
## INVESTING FOR DIVIDENDS

# High dividend portfolios

When I first gave advice to clients on their investment positions some 30 years ago, the first meeting was always a very long one during which we discussed all aspects of their financial lives. The range of possible financial solutions available to the clients was not quite so long as it would be today. In fact, it was very short. They could have a managed portfolio of shares in one of three categories:

1.  A high-risk portfolio seeking high levels of capital growth,

2.  a balanced portfolio seeking both income and capital growth, or

3.  a high-income, lower-risk portfolio.

Very simplistic compared to the choice on offer today, but just about fit for purpose at the time. When it came to their future portfolio many chose the high income and lower risk portfolio as their preferred option. Not surprising as both high income and low risk are very comfortable concepts. What was surprising is that during the 1980s and in the early 90s this type of portfolio, more often than not, achieved higher overall returns than the pure capital growth/high risk alternatives that were specifically managed to achieve higher returns!

This seemed very strange to me having been brought up on a staple diet of the risk/reward ratio. Contrary to this well established principle, clients with high dividend portfolios and a lower risk exposure actually also enjoyed the benefit of higher growth. In addition, there seemed to be a few other advantages of opting for the high dividend portfolio:

> "Clients with high dividend portfolios and a lower risk exposure actually also enjoyed the benefit of higher growth."

1.   Earnings growth and the resultant increase in dividends were far more consistent. By contrast, capital growth delivered by an increase in the share price in the short-term was, and still is, extremely volatile, unpredictable and unreliable.

2.   High dividend portfolios also delivered more immediate rewards. Capital growth for investors is always a long-term objective and very often requires patience. However, you receive dividends twice a year and provided you purchased cum dividend you could receive the first within a few months.

3.   It also seemed to produce a far more relaxed client. They did not tend to bother you for daily valuations and worry each time their shares fell in value on the markets; it was highly unlikely they felt that the companies they held shares in had just become less profitable just because the share price had fallen. In fact, over time it is fair to say these clients looked upon capital growth not as the raison d'etre of their portfolios, but as a very welcome by-product of the growth in income they sought.

## Defining the key terms

At this point let me quickly define some important terms in the world of earnings and dividends:

### earnings per share (EPS)

EPS is the net profit of a company divided by the number of its shares in issue. In other words, the proportion of net profit that is due to each share. For example, if in one year a company has a net profit of £20m and it has 100m share in issue, its EPS would be 20p (£20m/100m).

### earnings yield

The earnings yield is calculated by dividing the EPS by the share price (and then expressed as a percentage). The higher this figure, the better. For example, continuing the previous example, if a company has an EPS of 20p and a share price of 400p, then its earnings yield would be 5%.

Note: the earnings yield is the reciprocal of the PE (earnings yield = 1/PE). So, in this example, the company's PE would be 20x (1/5%).

### dividend

The dividend is the amount of a company's net earnings that are paid to shareholders (the rest of the earnings will be retained in the business to fund expansion, provide liquidity etc.).

### dividend yield

The dividend expressed as a percentage of the current share price. For example, if the dividend is 10p and the current share price is 400p, the dividend yield would be 2.5% (10p/400p).

### dividend cover

This is the term given to the relationship between the earnings per share and the dividend per share. It tells you how many times the dividend could be paid out of the current year's profits. It provides a view on the dividend sustainability, in other words, how comfortably a company can pay its dividend. For example, if dividend per share is 10p and EPS is 20p, then the dividend cover is two.

Once again, the higher the cover the better; ideally, I like to see levels of two or more.

You can find details of the earnings, dividend and dividend cover in the company accounts and on all the stockbroking websites. On the Barclays Stockbrokers website you will find it under the fundamentals tab in the financial sector. An extract showing these details for AstraZeneca is shown in the following screenshot.

## Figure 5.1: screenshot of Barclays stockbroker web page

| Continuing Operations | | | | | |
|---|---|---|---|---|---|
| PE Ratio - Adjusted | 7.4 | 8.8 | 7.9 | 11.4 | 15. |
| PEG - Adjusted | 0.3 | 0.5 | 0.6 | 0.3 | 0. |
| Earnings per Share Growth - Adjusted | 24% | 16% | 14% | 33% | 45% |
| Dividend Cover | 2.75 | 2.49 | 2.34 | 2.24 | 2.2 |
| Revenue per Share | 2,265.47¢ | 2,174.88¢ | 1,977.19¢ | 1,692.78¢ | 1,481.14 |
| Pre-Tax Profit per Share | 746.34¢ | 597.45¢ | 533.98¢ | 546.23¢ | 412.31 |
| Operating Margin | 35.19% | 28.94% | 27.38% | 31.03% | 27.15% |
| Return on Capital Employed | 88.97% | 106.60% | 67.20% | 63.57% | 52.69% |
| **Continuing & Discontinued Operations** | | | | | |
| PE Ratio - Adjusted | 7.4 | 8.8 | 7.9 | n/a | 15. |
| PEG - Adjusted | 0.3 | 0.5 | n/a | n/a | 0. |
| Earnings per Share Growth - Adjusted | 24% | 16% | n/a | -100% | 45% |
| Dividend Cover | (2.75) | 2.49 | 2.34 | n/a | 2.2 |
| Dividend Yield | (4.9%) | 4.6% | 5.4% | 3.9% | 2.8% |
| Dividend per Share Growth | 12.20% | 9.63% | 8.72% | 35.53% | 35.01% |
| Operating Cash Flow per Share | 810.70¢ | 601.65¢ | 502.34¢ | 491.88¢ | 417.01 |
| Cash Incr/Decr per Share | 389.09¢ | (104.34¢) | (88.70¢) | 131.39¢ | 61.16 |
| Net Asset Value per Share (exc. Intangibles) | (89.36¢) | (422.37¢) | (430.50¢) | 716.88¢ | 678.97 |
| Net Gearing | 5.54% | 47.52% | 62.86% | -38.42% | -60.40% |

# The importance of reinvesting dividends

The Barclays Equity and Gilt Study and other works have confirmed the importance of the reinvested dividend when it comes to the long-term performance of shares. In the long-term it can make up a surprisingly significant proportion of the overall return. If you have not seen similar figures on this subject then you will find them surprising.

If you take figures from 1945 in the UK market to January 2010 then the difference in returns is huge. In real terms (taking into account inflation) a portfolio of £100 would have grown to £241 ignoring the dividends, while reinvesting the dividend the figure would be £4011.[3] A 16-fold increase!

| | 1945 | 2010 |
|---|---|---|
| Value of portfolio – divs not reinvested | £100 | £241 |
| Value of portfolio – divs reinvested | £100 | £4011 |

---

[3] Barclays Equity and Gilt Study 2010, see Figures 49 & 50.

Now, admittedly these figures are very long-term (65 years) and they are calculated using gross dividends, but nevertheless quite clearly they confirm the importance of the dividend to the long-term investor. The larger the dividend, the greater the potential impact.

## Dogs of the Dow – a portfolio with bite

I wonder now why I did not write this book 25 years ago based on these observations in the 1980s. It could have made me famous like it did a Mr O'Higgins.

The cult of the high-dividend share was without doubt well established in this country long before 1991, but it was in this year in his book *Beating the Dow* that Michael O'Higgins converted it into an investment strategy that became known as the *Dogs of the Dow*. In this publication he advocated investing each year in the top ten yielding shares in the Dow Jones Industrial Average Index (DJIA), which comprises the 30 largest companies in the USA. Many of these offered high yields because of recent share price weakness – hence the term "dog" applied.

The main reasons for the popularity of the concept were that it was simple and reasonably effective. I find many investors' expectations are not that high and most would settle for this combination. For example, from 1972 to 2007 returns of the Dog followers would have averaged 12.6% a year, beating the Dow by about 10%[4].

Dividends are normally associated with mature companies, and by restricting himself to just the 30 companies in the Dow Index, O'Higgins applied his strategy only to the bluest of blue chips. I think this is an important element of the plan, as it helps to reduce risk and volatility.

### Does 2008 invalidate the Dog theory?

However, in some years followers of the Dog stocks would have found themselves to be barking up the wrong tree. For instance, 2008 proved to be a terrible year as the epicentre of the crisis was the financial sector and many of the bank and insurance stocks at the time would have qualified for Dog status.

---

[4] Source: Michael O'Higgins as quoted in money.cnn.com.

Many clients lost faith in large-cap, high-dividend stocks at this time, not only because of the share price underperformance but also because many dividends were reduced or even suspended. Their confidence in this type of share was understandably undermined. However, I think you have to put 2008 into its correct context. You have to remember that we were dealing with once in a lifetime events that shook the financial markets to their very core. I have certainly not lived through times like this before and hope I don't again.

It is unwise in my opinion to allow such extreme events to significantly impact your long-term investment strategy. Learn from them (and see the later chapter on diversification), but don't let them shape your whole investment thinking.

As markets stabilised from mid-2009, things have begun to get back to something that resembles normal, and in 2010 the Dogs were back on top again.

Although the performance quoted previously is based on American markets and the strategy has US origins, there is a very strong correlation between the US Dogs and their UK canine cousins. Without doubt this whole concept has some value and an equal application in the UK.

## Three reasons why the Dogs strategy works

Despite significant underperformance in 2008 there is a sound investment logic why a high-dividend blue chip policy is one that should be given serious consideration by the long-term investor who is looking for a relatively low risk, low maintenance portfolio.

1.  A high dividend can sometimes be a sign that a stock has been oversold. The negative correlation between price and yield can mean that a stock which currently offers a high yield is cheap and has the capacity to recover.

2.  With Blue Chip stocks there has always been a propensity for dividends not to be reduced to reflect current weaker trading conditions. This tendency was reversed in the crash of 2008 when some companies took the opportunity to "kitchen sink" all their bad news. This included on occasions a reduction in the dividend. It is expected things will return slowly to normal as far as dividends are concerned. They are often viewed, especially with larger corporations, as an average measure of the value of the company and this makes the income element of the overall

returns far less volatile than the capital growth achieved via the share price.

3. The willingness of the management of the company to release significant amounts of profit in the form of a dividend to the shareholders, as opposed to retaining it in the business, can be viewed as a vote of confidence by them in the current financial status and future prospects of the company.

## Applying the Dogs strategy to the UK market

Applied to the FTSE100, the 30 largest companies is a list that will currently take you down to Eurasian Natural Resources Corporation (ENRC) with a market capitalisation at the time of writing of £13.8bn. Using the one year forecast dividend, which is the version I would prefer, the ten companies with the highest dividend yield, and therefore the current ten members of the *Dogs of the FTSE100*, are shown in the following table:

| Company | Div Yield(%) |
|---|---|
| National Grid | 6.9 |
| AstraZeneca | 5.2 |
| Vodafone | 5.2 |
| Royal Dutch Shell | 5.2 |
| GlaxoSmithKline | 5.0 |
| Imperial Tobacco Group | 4.9 |
| British America Tobacco | 4.8 |
| Centrica | 4.2 |
| BT Group | 4.1 |
| Unilever | 3.7 |

This constitutes a portfolio of large-cap stocks reasonably diversified with an average yield of 4.9%.

By using stock filters you can adjust or refine the search. For instance, if you used the current dividend yield instead of the one year forecast figure, the list would only change by one member. BP would take the place of Unilever. If you added a minimum dividend cover of two to the existing current yield list, only AstraZeneca with a dividend cover of 2.8, BT with cover of 2.7 and Imperial Tobacco of 2.1 would qualify. Using the one year forecast you would add Unilever with a striking dividend cover of 3.2 to the list.

### iShares FTSE UK Dividend Plus [IUKD]

If this strategy is of interest but you prefer to make a single investment in high-yielding stocks, then you might wish to consider an ETF: iShares FTSE UK Dividend Plus [IUKD]. In any case, it makes an interesting fund to study as it employs a high income strategy. It certainly represents a relatively cheap option. ETFs pay no stamp duty and this fund has a total expense ratio (TER) of just 0.40%. This fund provides exposure to the 50 highest yielding stocks within the FTSE 350 weighted by the one year forecast yield.

There are a few differences between this fund and a true Dogs of the Dow strategy:

1.  The first relates to the size of the companies involved. Although all are of reasonable size and perfectly liquid, some are minnows compared to the giants of the Dow. As indicated previously, I do think the size of a company is an important factor in the success of a high dividend policy and it may be harder to replicate the consistency using smaller companies.

2.  Michael O'Higgin's policy involved rebalancing the portfolio each year. The IUKD fund rebalances each six months. I prefer the latter. Perhaps the reasons why O'Higgins went for an annual change was driven by dealing costs that were much higher in those days and also because he used the annual yield. This brings me to the next point of difference.

3.  The IUKD fund uses the one year forecast dividend as opposed to the current year's dividend recommended by the Dogs of the Dow. Once again, I prefer the forecast option.

4.  The Dogs of the Dow involved ten equal investments, whereas the IUKD fund involves 50 unequal ones weighted by reference to the size of the forecast yield. I marginally prefer the former. There is a fine line between diversification and over-dilution. I think 50 stocks crosses this line.

The five-year chart of the ETF is shown next, which shows how badly a high dividend policy suffered in 2008. Over the next five years I expect a reversion to the norm. A good solid level of performance delivered by a simple strategy. Once again it passes my 3 Box Test!

**Figure 5.2: share price chart of iShares FTSE UK Dividend Plus [IUKD]**

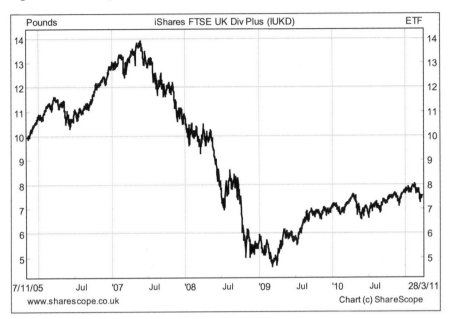

## My UK version of the Dogs of the Dow

My own version of the strategy for the UK market would retain some of the features of the original Dogs of the Dow Theory and some of the ETF. To summarise:

1.  I would retain the equal value of the constituent stocks, as opposed to weighting the investments in line with yields as the ETF does. I think this is necessary to pass the simplicity test.

2.  I would stick with just ten stocks to avoid smaller companies and over-dilution.

3.  I would use the one year forecast dividend as opposed to the current yield.

4.  The portfolio would be reviewed every six months as opposed to every year.

You can create your own updated list of Dog stocks very easily by using the stock filters on all the main stockbroker and financial websites. In the market cap section put in the minimum of £14bn and adjust it up and down until you get a sample of 30. In the forecast one year dividend yield put in a minimum of 3.5% and then pick the top ten!

## One final point – maiden dividends

On the subject of dividends, a stock selection technique that is interesting is investing in companies when they announce their maiden dividends.

Obviously, this involves what are normally small companies who may have moved into profit for the first time. The maiden dividend is obviously a plus for a stock in its own right as it creates another reason to hold a stock other than just hoping for the share price to rise. However, it is more than that. Stock market watchers see it almost as a declaration of confidence given by the board of directors on the sustainability and growth of the present profit levels and on the general financial strength of the company.

I came across this technique almost by accident. I noticed that shareholdings I owned when maiden dividends were announced did well not just for the few days after the announcement, as you would expect, but for many months and sometimes years after. Investing after the announcement will mean that you miss the first jump in price, but the beneficial impact on the share price often lasts much longer.

Recent examples that demonstrate how this can work are Medusa Mining [MML], Advanced Medical Solutions [AMS] and more recently Axis-Shield [ASD].

The following chart demonstrates the impact in the case of Medusa Mining. Obviously, there are many more influences on the price than simply the announcement of the first dividend, which in this case was made on the 28th October 2010, but there is no doubt in my mind it was one of the factors involved.

**Figure 5.3: share price chart of Medusa Mining [MML]**

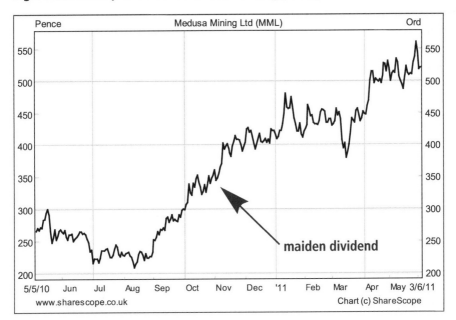

Although I found the technique by accident, I now use it actively to highlight possible investment opportunities. Another share selection method that I feel for me passes the 3 Box Test.

# Conclusion

The dividend may have gone out of fashion in the 90s as chasing pure capital growth seemed more rewarding in a decade that saw the FTSE100 climb over 4000 points, but subsequent events and the long-term figures show you ignore them at your cost. The greater consistency of the dividend growth makes it easier on occasions to be a shareholder and over the longer-term the contribution they make to the overall performance of your portfolio make them too important to ignore.

# CHAPTER 6:

## DIVERSIFICATION

An old English proverb:

*'don't put all your eggs in one basket'*

helps illustrate what diversification is all about in the investment world. The reduction of risk by the spreading of investments and avoiding having too much of your money in one place. Instead of a basket, in this context substitute one share, one sector, one country or one asset class.

This principle of diversification sits at the very core of investment management and a diversification policy successfully implemented is one of the main features that differentiate investment from gambling.

## A story of false diversification

I met a lady some years ago who had a substantial number of shares in one company, Barclays Bank. I spoke to her about the need to spread her investments. When the crash of 2008 came I thought of her and wondered if she had taken any steps to reduce her exposure.

I saw her again recently and took the opportunity to ask her if she had sold any of her shares in Barclays to diversify. I was delighted to learn that she had. However, I then learnt she had sold 50% of her Barclays holding and with the freed cash had purchased RBS and Lloyds! She had increased the number of companies she was exposed to, but had reinvested in very similar stocks within the same sector. She had spread her money but had not achieved any real diversification or reduced risk to any significant degree.

Diversification is not simply about buying more baskets. Astute investment demands it has to be invested into the right blend of assets to meet your needs and expose you to an appropriate level of risk. The mix of investments must also be guided by the prevailing value in the different market segments. Successful investment, therefore, is very often about focus as well as divergence.

There are three different levels at which I think the investor should seek to diversify:

1.  Asset class

2.  Geography

3.  Sectors and stock

# Asset allocation

Asset allocation should be about achieving a balance in your personal wealth, and usually involves spreading your wealth between the four main asset classes – namely cash, bonds, shares and property. This is a process you need to complete long before you even begin to think about what shares you are going to buy.

### Property

Those who own their own properties already have this asset class covered, provided they own a reasonable level of equity (i.e. the value of the property less mortgage outstanding). For those who don't own a property, exposure can be achieved with REITs (Real Estate Investment Trusts) and including these as part of the share portfolio.

Would it worry me as a home owner that my asset allocation is distorted so much by the disproportionate value of my house? No, it wouldn't, as the house is a home as well as an investment. However, I would not think of investing in another property until I had wealth in cash, bonds and shares equal in value to the equity in my existing property.

### Commodities

The range of asset classes in your financial plan could be increased from four to five, if you wanted to add commodities.

Personally, I would not fragment the asset allocation further by adding another category. Instead, I would simply include exposure to commodities as part of the share portfolio [see later chapter].

For the rest of this section I will be referring to the three main asset classes: cash, shares and bonds.

## The requirements of a portfolio

I have spoken to thousands of clients over the years and when I ask them what they are looking for from their invested capital almost all of them come up with the following list:

1. Liquidity (flexibility/access/cash reserve),

2 stability (protection/guarantees),

3. capital growth (bigger return),

4. income (if not now, then in the future), and

5. tax efficiency.

Let's look at each of the five in turn and which elements of an asset allocation portfolio can help:

1. **Cash deposit accounts** are the best provider of *liquidity*. They provide easy access to your money and little risk of losing your original deposit.

2. **Bonds** (gilts and corporate) would normally be the best provider of *stability* as they are guaranteed by the issuer (government or company).

3. **Shares** will be the best provider of *capital growth* in the long-term (as you will have seen from the figures in the first chapter). This class involves higher risk as the returns will depend on the performance of the company and the economy in which it operates.

4. **Income**. This is an interesting feature of all three main asset classes; each class has a different *income* pattern. Cash deposit accounts produce an income that will vary with interest rates (up and down). Bonds, once invested, are designed to provide a stable and regular (fixed) income. While shares tend to produce a rising income over the longer-term. The mix of all three is normally a good combination for the income-seeking investor, as each will be strong at different times, which is the real purpose of diversification. Income from cash will tend to be better in the short-term in times of rising or high interest rates, income from bonds will tend to be better in the short-term in times of falling and low interest rates, and income from shares will tend to be better in the long-term. By diversifying across the three asset classes you should have all bases covered.

5. **Tax efficiency**. All three asset classes can be invested in the UK inside ISAs and SIPPs, making them free from all personal taxes in the hands of a UK resident.

# The need for balance

*The big question is obviously: how should one divide one's money between cash, shares and bonds?*

In practice, the balance between the three main asset classes is dictated by many factors, but most relate to the individual's personal circumstances and preferences; for example, their age, risk appetite and income requirements.

On this subject I was once given some guidance by an elderly lady in Yorkshire during a Q&A session after an evening seminar. She told me, and the listening audience, in a blunt Sheffield accent to simply:

> take your age off 100 and invest this percentage in the stock market,
> then invest the balance equally between cash and bonds.

This is actually a fairly common rule of thumb; and perfectly reasonable it is too for a simple formula. However, while I do like simple things, it is lacking in two areas:

1. It ignores a person's risk profile, which I don't think is entirely dictated by age.

2. It does not take into account prevailing market conditions and valuations.

The second point seems to be very often overlooked.

## Assessing the prevailing market

I was perfectly happy to invest in corporate bonds back in March 2009, when yields on investment grade bonds in some segments was over 9%. I am less so today with redemption yields averaging 5.5%. UK gilts are even less attractive. With redemption yields averaging 3.1% below the level of inflation, they are priced to lose money. Eventually, gilt prices will fall and yields will rise; when that happens I will be happy to buy them so that they can perform their normal stabilising role in my portfolio. But at current prices and yields? Not for me, thank you.

A good way to get an overview of the bond markets is through a couple of ETFs. The following chart is of iShares iBoxx Sterling Corporate Bond [SLXX], which gives a good insight into the corporate bond market in the UK:

## Figure 6.1: chart of iShare iBoxx Sterling Corporate Bond [SLXX]

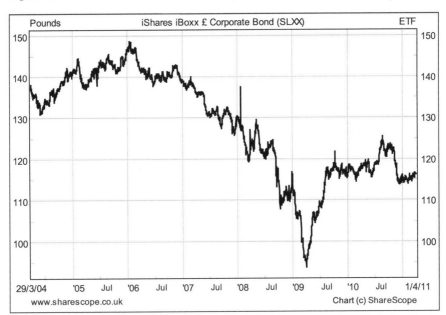

The following chart of iShares FTSE UK All Stocks Gilt [IGLT] provides a similar view of the UK gilt market:

## Figure 6.2: chart of FTSE UK All Stocks Gilt [IGLT]

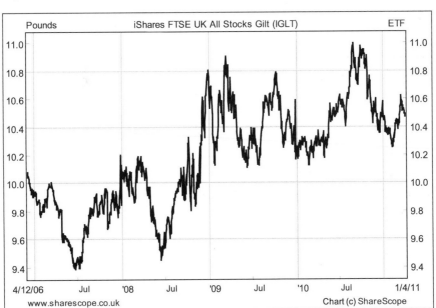

These two charts are interesting as, although gilts and bonds are placed in the same category when it comes to asset allocation and are similar in most respects, they show how they reacted very differently to the financial crisis of 2008/9.

The first chart shows the performance of the sample of investment grade corporate bonds held within this particular ETF, and shows how the price of the bonds fell dramatically until the summer of 2009 when they started to recover. Obviously, as the price of these corporate bonds fell sharply their income yields rose significantly – the yield on this particular ETF rose to a peak of 9%. An amazing level in view of the fact that the UK base rate was close to zero at 0.5%. Since then, prices have risen and income yields fallen to more normal levels (about 5% today).

In contrast, at the same time as the prices of corporate bonds were falling, the price of gilts did the opposite and rose sharply with yields falling to record low levels.

*Why?*

Risk, which seemed to be the only thing undervalued in previous years, became the focus of investors' attention. Investors were concerned about some companies' ability to repay their loans and pay the interest on them, therefore their value in the markets fell. Investors asked themselves whether companies would be able meet their future financial obligations. Fear in the markets was so high at the time, many thought the answer was no! Gilts are lower risk than corporate bonds as they are guaranteed by the government as opposed to a company. As risk became the main point of focus for investors they sought the relative safety of gilts; investors seemed prepared to pay any price for it. In other words, investors became more focused on the return of their capital rather than the return on it.

## Dynamically managing asset allocation

Asset allocation has traditionally been regarded as a fairly static and long-term process. However, due to the increased levels of volatility in the markets illustrated in these charts, I believe that a more dynamic value-based approach needs to be adopted.

For me, in 2011 this means that despite the fact I normally manage my portfolio with a traditional three-piece asset allocation, I will not be holding any gilts until prices fall and yields rise. I have also now reduced my corporate bond exposure until valuations change. By contrast, I will increase my holding of blue chip equities as they should produce more income and add a little growth into the equation.

This does not mean I will ignore cash, even though interest rates are at rock bottom. Holding cash has never been about the return for me because as a long-term investment all the figures show it just simply does not work. I will hold cash for the flexibility and time it gives me. The flexibility to feed money into markets if and when their values become compelling; and the time to wait for the growth of long-term investments. It's all about balance. Holding a cash balance means I am never a forced seller of a long-term investment at a bad time in the market. However, you need to make sure you do not hold too much as it will simply dilute the performance of your overall portfolio. In normal circumstances I find that holding about 10% of the portfolio value in cash is the right level for me. If the Rule of 20 tells me to hold more then I would be comfortable doing so.

# Global diversification

After you have addressed the fundamental question of your asset allocation, something to think about is the geographical exposure of your share portfolio.

It has always been regarded as sensible for the UK-based investor to include some international exposure in his or her portfolio. This is especially true at the moment, when the performance of the UK economy is expected to be lacklustre over the next few years.

In fact, the FTSE100 already gives reasonable international exposure as around 70% of all the earnings of FTSE100 companies originate from overseas. Despite this, I believe a significant proportion of your portfolio should be invested in overseas markets.

The way you achieve this is a harder question to answer than whether you should do it in the first place.

## Individual companies

You can invest direct in individual companies on overseas markets. Most brokers offer online dealing at very cheap rates. The problem with this option is that it is difficult to achieve the balance you need in every market. In addition, I find overseas markets are more difficult to research.

You may therefore decide to invest via a collective investment. There are two options: you can choose a tracker or an actively managed fund.

## Exchange traded funds

You can track overseas markets by using ETFs. They are usually very cheap and effective trackers. The range of ETFs is now very wide and they offer great flexibility when it comes to looking for international exposure. For example, there are ETFs that offer exposure to individual countries, such as:

- iShares MSCI Australia

- db x-trackers FTSE/Xinhua China 25

- Lyxor ETF MSCI Korea

Or there are ETFs offering exposure to regions, such as:

- CS ETF MSCI EM Latin America

- Lyxor ETF East Europe

- iShares MSCI Pacific ex-Japan

Or there are ETFs offering exposure to themes, such as:

- iShares S&P Global Water

- Lyxor ETF MSCI World Health Care

- PowerShares Global Agriculture

The alternative to trackers such as ETFs is actively managed funds.

## Managed funds

Unit trusts, OEICs and investment trusts are the main options in this space. These are serious alternatives even though this book is written for the self-directed investor. Obviously, if you choose to use them you will be delegating management on this portion of your portfolio to a fund manager.

The case for this becomes stronger if you have faith in a particular manager, or a fund's theme is one you especially like, or ideally a combination of both.

For example, I like the Fidelity Chinese Special Situations fund [FCSS] – the fund focuses on the domestic expansion in China, which is a theme I believe will be a profitable one to invest in, and it is managed by the renowned Anthony Bolton. He has not only come out of semi-retirement to manage this fund but has also moved to Hong Kong and invested a significant amount of his personal wealth in the fund. Commitment at this level by someone of his status should not be ignored.

I think overseas investment is an essential part of any portfolio. At present, for example, I have exposure to the USA, Brazil, China and Canada via ETFs, investment trusts and unit trusts.

# Sectors and stocks

### 10/2/20 Rule

It's important to get a balanced spread within your equity investments at an individual sector and stock level. I use a simple guideline to help get the necessary balance right, which I refer to as the *10/2/20 Rule*:

1.   I don't put more than 10% of my equity portfolio money into one share.

2.   I don't invest in more than 2 stocks in any one sector.

3.   I don't want more than 20 stocks in my portfolio.

I know many investors who ignored these rules but have learnt a hard lesson. Over-exposure to the banks and other financial stocks in 2008 and 2009, followed by the BP disaster in the Mexican Gulf the following year, taught people the risks of over-concentration in a few stocks or sectors. This is true even for blue chip stocks that appeared to have a reliable flow of revenue and profits.

Following the first two elements of this rule will not mean I avoid all the pain, but it will limit the damage. It also means that I will always have a minimum of ten stocks in my portfolio. However, share diversification can be overdone.

### The limits of diversification

As a general rule I would not want more than 20 stocks in my investment portfolio. If I am not confident enough to put at least 5% of my money into a company then I should simply not invest in it. Less than 5% means that you will be investing in companies that are outside your top 20. I believe you need to be more focused than this. Firstly, it is difficult to analyse more than 20 companies; second, fragmentation can simply mean you dilute performance. In addition, if you invest in too many companies, your portfolio can begin to match the performance of an index such as the FTSE100 (your portfolio effectively becomes what is sometimes called a *closet tracker fund*), at which point you might as well just buy a straightforward tracker fund and save yourself the time and cost of investing in individual shares.

This 5% rule applies to investments only. Sometimes for short-term trades, especially in small cap stocks, smaller amounts can be appropriate. I also think it wise to build and reduce holdings rather than just buy them in one block deal, so there will be occasions when I buy (and sell) shares less than the 5% figure.

# Your risk profile

There is a danger that investors can sometimes become too obsessed by the process of investing in individual shares, that they lose track of where their overall exposure is. It's like working on a jigsaw: while you have to look carefully at the individual pieces, it is important to always bear in mind the big picture. So, having got down to individual shares, let's now pull back to think about the overall risk of a portfolio.

### Risk/return

There is a relationship between a portfolio's risk and its returns: higher returns normally come from taking on higher risk. A consequence of this is that low-risk portfolios tend to have lower returns.

Now, imagine when assessing your overall risk appetite you have a risk ladder that has ten rungs. Rung one represents no risk (if there is such a thing!), the tenth rung is the highest risk possible.

*Where on this ladder would you stand?*

This is an important question only you can answer. If you are on the first rung that is fine, providing you appreciate the consequences of that decision (i.e. that you could expect almost no return on your portfolio). If you are on the top rung, you have the potential for great gains – and losses.

## Assessing the risk of your portfolio

For most investors I speak to, a risk rating somewhere between four and eight is common. However, there is often a difference between their assessment of their risk appetite and the actual risk position of their portfolio. This can happen for many reasons. It could be that the portfolio was built up in a piecemeal fashion over many years, or it could be due to a lack of understanding of risk.

A good starting point is assessing your own risk appetite on a scale of one to ten (one lowest, ten highest). Then calculate the rating of your overall portfolio by using the following risk grades. This will provide a very simple method of comparing your risk appetite with the overall risk rating of your portfolio. The table is very crude, but it is a simple starting point to analyse a portfolio's risk.

| Risk rating | Asset types |
| --- | --- |
| 1 (low) | cash, gilts |
| 2 | gilt funds, corporate bonds |
| 3 | corporate bond funds, absolute return funds |
| 4 | unit trusts, OEICs, ETFs backed by physical assets |
| 5 | large cap shares |
| 6 | mid cap shares, investment trusts and REITS |
| 7 | small cap shares |
| 8 | ETCs, covered warrants |
| 9 | leveraged ETFs/ ETCs |
| 10 (high) | CFDs and FSTs |

To give a simple illustration, if an investor had an equal four-way split of money in large cap shares, mid cap shares, ETFs and gilts they would have a rating of four,

$$(5+6+4+1)/4 = 4$$

Don't regard this as a scientific equation. Just calculate the figure in approximate terms by using the numbers and average them on a proportional basis by value. The questions I could raise on this table would certainly outnumber the investments available, but I have deliberately kept away from the detail. What it loses in detail, hopefully it gains in clarity.

Another simple example to aid understanding: somebody who assesses their overall risk rating as a seven, but whose portfolio is equally split between cash, corporate bond funds and large cap stocks. They rate themselves a seven and yet, according to my calculations, they have a portfolio with an overall rating of three,

$$(1+3+5)/3 = 3$$

A rating of three would be about right for a very cautious investor, but not for an adventurous one. I am not suggesting that they should immediately sell all their investments and switch into covered warrants, but they should be aware of the divergence between their intention and their actual portfolio.

What concerns me is that I come across many investors who can give me chapter and verse on the investment attractions of a particular AIM stock, but have not given their overall risk rating a second thought. They have their investment priorities in the wrong order like someone with gangrene in their leg obsessing about getting their toenails cut!

Another area of concern would be when clients do have an appreciation of their overall risk appetite, and also of the risk rating of their actual portfolio, but because of this they do not consider investments that do not fit on an individual basis. For example, cautious investors will rule out ever looking at a large range of investments because of their perceived higher risk.

But it is not the risk of individual investments that is important; rather, it is the risk of the overall portfolio. They should focus on the overall mix rather than the individual risk ratings of each investment. It is a bit like making a curry – whether you prefer them mild or red hot, often the basic ingredients remain the same, the only difference is the balance of spices added to the dish. So do not be put off by individual options that would normally be outside your target area, just make sure that the overall blend suits your risk palate. Instead of restricting the range of risk of the investments held in your portfolio, think about controlling the risk via the level of cash you hold. The higher risk you are, the lower your cash reserve needs to be. If for any reason your appetite for risk falls then simply increase your level of cash. It might be regarded as a crude method of risk management by the purists, but it gives a method of control that is simple, effective and instant.

# CHAPTER 7:

## DIRECTORS' DEALS

There are many ways to pick winning shares, and each way has its share of supporters and detractors. However, when it comes to following directors' deals, it is difficult to find many detractors.

## What are directors' deals?

This refers to the buying or selling of shares in a company by directors of the company itself.

Trading based on insider information is of course illegal, but directors can deal in their own shares provided the deals are reported appropriately to the regulators. Details of such trades are then issued to the public each trading day.

There are certain times in the trading year when such transactions are not allowed. These are called *closed periods*; these normally last for two months prior to the release of the company accounts.

I believe it makes sense to keep such transactions under very close inspection as, in theory, directors should know their business better than any outside investor.

### Actions or words?

The phrases we use in our everyday language give a clue to the significance of these deals:

*'put your money where your mouth is'*
*'actions speak louder than words'*

Those are just two that spring to mind that illustrate why people place such importance upon these transactions. Words are cheap, and stock measurement methods can always be questioned. But investors do take notice when directors take money out of their own wallets and buy their own company shares at their full market value; it is the ultimate action that corporate insiders can take to indicate confidence in their company.

Even if you take the view that the directors are totally information neutral on their company's shares and they just happen to be cash rich at the time, the deals would still be of significance because of the number of stock market watchers who think they are. To a degree they become a self-fulfilling prophecy. If a director buys shares in his company, investors will believe that one of the reasons he does that is because he thinks the shares are undervalued; so investors buy them for this reason and the share price rises.

# Not every deal is the same

However, directors' dealings do require some analysis, and not every deal has the same significance.

I regard share purchases as a far more reliable positive indicator than a sale is a negative one. There are many personal reasons why a director may sell shares. For example, he may want the money to buy a house, or to pay some bills, or he may feel he just has too much exposure to one company (considering that his salary and, possibly, pension will also depend on this same company).

I am not saying for one moment that a significant director's sale is anything other than a negative on a stock. The research clearly confirms that it is and the market really does not like to see it. What I am saying, though, is that in my experience directors' purchases are a far better and reliable buying signal than a director's disposal of shares is a selling one. I always take note of purchases, I have an email alert sent to me listing them on a daily basis, and always include them as one of the criteria when I am using stock filters.

So I believe directors' purchases are far more important to watch out for than sales. However, without doubt, some purchases are more important than others.

## Categorising directors' deals

The following factors need to be considered when analysing the significance of any directors' deals:

### 1. Size of deal

The higher the value of the deal, the more significant it is. Obviously, if a director buys £500,000 of his company's shares, that is more significant than if he bought only £5000.

## 2. Size of company

It is more significant if directors of small companies buy their own shares, than directors of large companies. Large, diversified companies are difficult to value by anyone – including corporate insiders. To paraphrase Donald Rumsfeld, there is a feeling there are less known unknowns or there are only unknown unknowns and these remain unknown even to the directors!

The other reason why the size of the company is important is the impact of the actual deals. Take a big blue chip like Vodafone, the volume of deals that are placed on the market in a day can be a thousand times more than even a mid cap stock.

## 3. Number of directors involved

I think this is even more important than the value of the deals. When only one director buys shares, it may be interesting. But when a group of directors make significant purchases at the same time in a small cap stock, it's time to sit up and take notice. There is no doubt in my mind that deals done by groups of directors influence the market more. When one director buys, the motive to do the deal could simply be personal, but when more than one director is involved the reason is always seen to be company specific.

### Check the price of the deal

*Has the deal been carried out at the full market value?*

When a deal is reported, so is the price at which the deal was transacted. Make sure it's been carried out at the full market price and it's not simply the exercise of a discounted option. These details are shown on all the stockbrokers' websites and updated daily.

# Following directors' dealings in practice

So what you need to watch out for is a group of directors of a small company buying significant amounts of shares in their company over relatively short time periods at the full market value.

*Sounds OK, but does the theory convert into practice?*

Research from directorsdeals.com has shown that it does. Their study showed that shares bought by directors increased on average 23.5% while those they sold fell in value by an average 15.5% over a one-year period following the transaction.

Obviously, a good way to judge the effectiveness of following directors' dealings is to look at a few price charts and inspect the price action after any deals. So, let's look at some examples:

# Examples

### 1. Communisis [CMS]

This is a marketing services provider that is going through a restructuring plan. From November 2009 to February 2010 there were ten separate directors' purchases all at their full market value. Although only one, when viewed in isolation, was for what I would regard as a significant amount (£49,000), the fact there were ten separate transactions from five different directors in a 15-week period from November 2009 to February 2010 was significant. The following chart shows that the share price has doubled since the time of these ten directors' purchases.

**Figure 7.1: share price chart of Communisis**

## Table 7.1: directors' deals in Communisis

| Chart legend | Date | Directors' deal |
|---|---|---|
| A | 11/11/2009 | Andy Blundell – Buy 50,000 shares at 19p |
| B | 03/12/2009 | Peter Hickson – Buy 50,000 shares at 17p |
| C | 09/12/2009 | Peter Hickson – Buy 50,000 shares at 15p |
| D | 18/12/2009 | Peter Hickson – Buy 100,000 shares at 14p |
| E | 24/12/2009 | John Wells – Buy 25,000 shares at 14p |
| F | 31/12/2009 | Alistair Blaxill – Notification of Holding; |
| G | 25/02/2010 | John Wells – Buy 20,000 shares at 14p<br>Peter Hickson – Buy 350,000 shares at 14p<br>Roger W Jennings – Buy 30,000 shares at 14p |
| H | 26/02/2010 | John Wells – Buy 15,000 shares at 15p<br>Michael Graham Firth – Buy 100,000 shares at 15p |

## 2. Kofax [KFX]

This company is a data capture specialist. The shares are not cheap with a PE of 20, but its PEG is attractive at 0.7. The purchases here were made by four directors at the full market value within an eight-week period from November 2010 to December 2010. The amounts involved were also substantial, totalling over £350,000. The following chart confirms the details and confirms that the share price has risen over 20% since the first deals were reported, hopefully with more to come.

## Figure 7.2: share price chart of Kofax

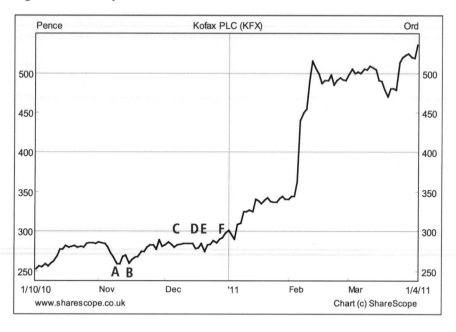

## Table 7.2: director's deals in Kofax

| Chart legend | Date | Directors' dealings |
|---|---|---|
| A | 10/11/2010 | Christopher J Conway – Buy 15,000 shares at 260p |
| B | 11/11/2010 | Greg Lock – Buy 57,429 shares at 272p |
| C | 09/12/2010 | Joe Rose – Buy 10,000 shares at 285p |
| D | 21/12/2010 | Martyn Christian – Buy 30,000 shares at 281p |
| E | 22/12/2010 | Martyn Christian – Buy 5000 shares at 281p |
| F | 31/12/2010 | Martyn Christian – Buy 10,000 shares at 301p |

## 3. Salamander Energy [SMDR]

This Asia-focused oil company is forecast to move back into profit in 2011 and has been the subject of various pieces of positive news flow in recent months. In mid-January 2011, three directors purchased shares at the full market value aggregating in value to over £500,000. The following chart shows the details. It's obviously too early to record any price movement but it will be interesting to see whether the price reacts positively as I would expect following these transactions.

**Figure 7.3: share price chart of Salamander Energy**

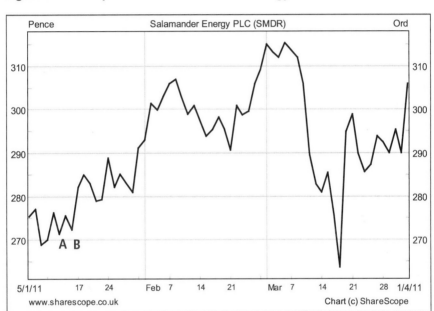

**Table 7.3: director's deals in Salamander Energy**

| Chart legend | Date | Directors' dealings |
|---|---|---|
| A | 13/01/2011 | Robert Cathery – Buy 100,000 shares at 273p<br>Michael James Pavia – Buy 10,000 shares at 271p |
| B | 14/01/2011 | Charles Jamieson – Buy 75,000 shares at 276p |

If you look back a little further you can find some dramatic examples of share price growth that were preceded by directors buying their own company shares. Let's go back just less than two years for two examples.

In March 2009, two directors purchased shares in the Volex group [VLX] at 24p. They invested a total of just over £34,000. Not that large an amount (and I imagine they wish they had bought more as since this date the shares have risen 15-fold to £3.60!).

**Figure 7.4: share price chart of Volex**

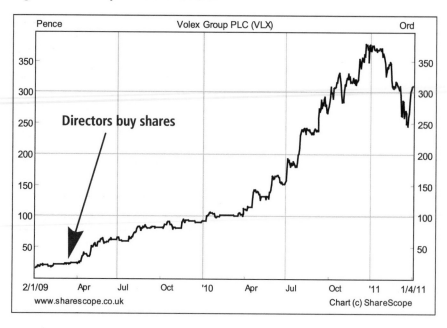

In April 2009, three directors of Petra Diamonds [PDL] bought shares in the company. They invested a total of £910,000 at 22p; since then the share price has risen eight-fold to £1.78.

**Figure 7.5: share price chart of Petra Diamonds**

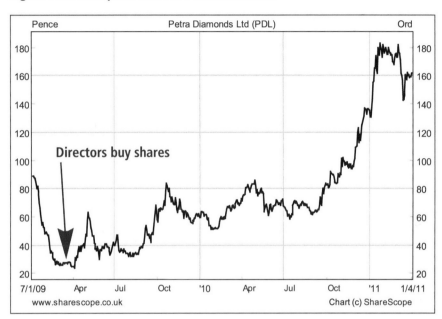

## Conclusion

I believe that directors' purchases made at the full market price can be a positive sign for the share price, and can be used by investors and traders. They become an even more positive sign when the amount of money involved is significant, the company is small and there is more than one director involved. It's a share selection method that ticks all my boxes.

Details of directors' dealings are freely available; I would encourage you to set up a daily email alert, a service which most brokers offer at no extra charge.

# CHAPTER 8:
## CHARTING THE WAY

## Fundamentalists v. technicians

Stock market analysts tend to fall into two camps. By far the larger group are known as *fundamentalists*; they focus on the business fundamentals of a company and the wider economy. They will study balance sheets, news flows and brokers' opinions and will use tools such as the PE, dividend yield and PEG to analyse companies. The second group are known as *technical analysts*, or *chartists*. They attempt to forecast the future direction of share prices through the study of past price behaviour. To achieve this, the sole object of their attention is the chart.

In this chapter I will look into the basics of technical analysis and try to answer some simple questions. Although, personally, I stand firmly in the fundamentalist camp, I will also explain why and how I use charts to help me implement some of my fundamental investment strategies. Many books (some very large!) have been written on this subject, so in this one chapter I will obviously be dealing with this subject with the lightest of touches.

If you listen to two technical analysts discussing the market, you may be excused if you feel that you have been secretly transported to another planet. Their conversation may well include references to Ichimoku clouds, Stochastics, Elliot waves and dead cat bounces!

It is very easy, therefore, for both experienced and novice investors alike to simply dismiss such analysts as stock market geeks. But I believe it would be wrong to label technical analysis (TA) as an area for anorak investors only. Even the most traditional investor who has been brought up on a staple diet of price earnings ratios may find that using certain aspects of technical analysis may improve his or her investment performance.

# Three principles of technical analysis

The three most quoted principles that underpin technical analysis, and which are often used to justify its value, are:

## 1. Everything is in the price

This results from an academic theory called the Efficient Market Hypothesis (EMH). This hypothesis proposes that the current price of a share reflects all the knowable information about that share. If, for example, there was some new information anywhere about a company, then traders will buy or sell the shares on the basis of that information and the shares will immediately adjust in price to fully reflect that information. If one believes in the EMH (and many people don't) then the logical conclusion is that there is no point in analysing the fundamentals of a company, because anything you find is already *in the price*. And, hence, the only sensible thing to study is the price itself.

## 2. Prices move in trends

Look at any chart and more likely than not you will see periods in which the price tends to fairly steadily move upwards or downwards. Many traders (and shorter-term investors) believe that the way to make money is to spot these price trends and jump on them and ride them until they change. In fact, a common saying in trading circles is *the trend is your friend*.

Trends can be a very attractive proposition. For a start, they do definitely exist – one can see them on charts. It looks an easy way to make money. The problem is that in real-time it can be difficult to know when a trend is ending or just pausing for breath.

## 3. History repeats itself

The idea here is the prices behave in similar ways to how they have done in the past.

This basically is the principle that sustains the whole concept of support and resistance levels about which I will write later. The concept basically is that the price of a stock index or commodity will react to price rises or falls in the future the same way as it had done in the past.

Take a look at the following chart of GlaxoSmithKline.

**Figure 8.1: share price chart of GlaxoSmithKline [GSK]**

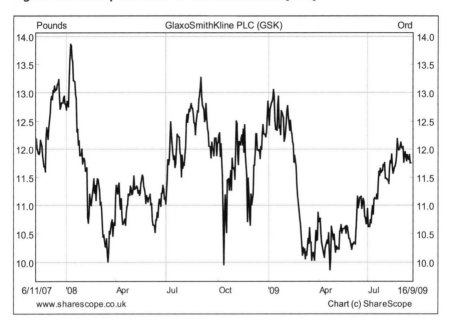

You can see that in early 2008 the price was falling and then bounced off the £10 level. A few months later, in October 2008, a similar thing happened. And then in early 2009, the price fell to just above the £10 level and bounced around there for a while before rising back to £12.

The price didn't seem to want to fall below £10! If the price subsequently started to fall, while there is no guarantee it would not fall below £10, it seems reasonable to suppose that there's a better than 50% chance the price would again bounce off the £10 level. As I said, there's no guarantee this would happen, but the previous price behaviour at this level might be enough to make traders (and investors) think twice before *selling* Glaxo shares at the £10 level, and may encourage others to position themselves ready to jump in quickly and *buy* the shares if the price again looks like it is going to bounce off that £10 level. This being the case makes it even more likely that the price will react in this manner!

The preceding is an example of a charting pattern called a *support level*. There are many such patterns in technical analysis, which all rely on this idea that price behaviour patterns repeat themselves.

# Does charting work?

The big question is: does technical analysis work?

For every study that supports TA you can find one that does not. So there is therefore little point asking an expert; therefore I feel more than qualified to give you a view.

Even if TA cannot accurately predict future price movements, I believe it can help to identify and verify trading opportunities. Importantly, it can also add discipline to both your buy and sell decisions.

Investing is not all about trying to find the new wonder share that will make you a fortune (although that would be nice!); it is also about exiting a share with most of your profits intact or limiting your loss on a trade that did not work. Anything that helps give you a discipline for opening and closing positions is valuable.

### The shorter the time frame, the stronger the case

The shorter your investment time horizon, the more important TA becomes. This is why day, swing and trend traders use TA far more than long-term investors. Warren Buffett, and his mentor before him, Benjamin Graham, both spoke about how prices in the market would react differently over different time periods. They referred to the market in the short-term being a voting machine and in the long-term being a weighing machine. In other words, in the short-term, momentum could take the price of a security in any direction, but in the long-term the fundamentals will reassert themselves.

The view that value is the key long-term driver of price from two dyed-in-the wool fundamentalists is hardly surprising. However, in the short-term, they admit it's different. Price movements become more fickle and apparently random, and when trying to forecast short-term price direction current momentum should not be ignored.

### The trend is your friend

As a long-term investor who follows the fundamentals, and is a big fan of Warren Buffett, you would not expect me to be an avid follower of TA. However, I think it is a foolhardy investor who entirely dismisses the subject. For me, it will never be the prime investment tool, but without doubt it helps me to time my entries and exits.

Even if I had never read a word on TA, my experience of investing over the last three decades would have taught me one lesson: never knowingly invest against the direction of the existing price trend. This means that if a price is falling, avoid buying it. Even if the PEG is screaming value, I will try to wait until there is evidence that the existing downward trend has ended.

> "Most successful investors I know are not the ones who make the most right decisions; they are the ones who make the fewest mistakes."

This does not mean you cannot "be greedy when others are fearful". You can still buy shares at large discounted prices. It just means you won't buy a share at the all-time low. It should be noted, however, that most successful investors I know are not the ones who make the most right decisions; they are the ones who make the fewest mistakes.

# Case studies

Let me provide two examples to illustrate the point I am making: the first involves a stock I was looking to buy but the trend was down, and the second concerns a stock I am looking to sell but the trend is still up.

### 1. Cookson Group [CKSN]

This engineering and ceramics group is a member of the FTSE 350; it was a share that I had owned for a while some years ago so I felt it was in my "circle of confidence".

On 26th April 2010, the company announced that in response to a global increase in steel production it expected trading profits for the company for the first half of 2010 to come in at about £110m, approximately 20% higher than they were for the second half of 2009. The price had fallen a long way from its peak of £13.17 in October 2007. At the time of the announcement it was priced at about £5.60. The forecast PEG after the announcement was a very tempting 0.1. I wanted to buy. The only problem was the downward trend in the share price was still in place.

Although I wanted to buy the stock immediately, I was equally determined not to do so until the downtrend had changed.

It's not easy sometimes as the fear of buying too early is often finely balanced with the dread of buying too late.

As you can see from the following chart, the downward trend continued much further than fair value would have dictated (as it often does), until it reached a low of £3.67 in July 2010. You can see from the chart that the low was preceded and followed by a number of other similar troughs that had created a support level between the end of May to the end of August.

The exact timing of the purchase is a personal decision, but was dictated for me by the 30- and 90-day moving average [as I will explain later in this chapter]. Some may say that this is too late as I bought on the 17 August 2010 when the price was £4.51. That may be the case for a short-term trader, but for the long-term investor like myself I am convinced it's the right approach. Suffice to say at this juncture it was the downward trend that prevented me from buying too early and stopped me jumping in too early.

**Figure 8.2: share price chart of Cookson Group**

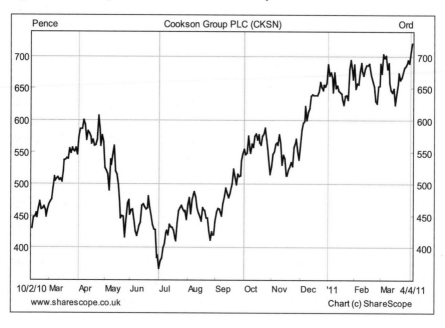

## 2. ASOS [ASC]

I am fast becoming an ASOS obsessive as I have written about this stock many times in previous publications as well as earlier in this book. However, it is such a good example of an upward trend delaying the sale I feel I must use it again!

I won't go through the whole history of my personal involvement with this stock as these details are included in an earlier chapter. Here, I want to focus on the sale not the purchase.

I have already said it was the PEG that was the main reason I bought the stock. As this rose (became less attractive) above one it no longer qualified as a GARP stock; and as it rose further it moved on to my watch list to sell. When the PEG rose to over two I sold half, and when it rose to 2.2 I sold another half of the remaining half. This has left me at the time of writing with 25% of the original holding. This stock has now got an amazingly expensive forward PE of 68 and a PEG of 2.3.

I am in no doubt about the quality of this company, but I am even more certain that the share is currently over-priced at £19 – yet I still hold 25% of the original holding.

*Why?*

Because the upward trend is still in existence. The following charts, over five-year and one-year periods, clearly illustrate the dilemma. When the fundamentals are shouting sell and the trend is screaming hold I listen to both. I think it is the only way to achieve a win-win situation.

You could, and when I am busy I often do, use a trailing stop order to sell to execute the deal when the price of the share falls by a specific amount from its previous peak. This is normally quite effective as it will sell when the price falls by the amount you set, and the price falling would often signal the end of the upward trend. In this particular case, this approach would not have worked as the share twice fell over 200 points before it resumed its upward trend. Sometimes it does seem the market is out to get you!

## Figure 8.3: share price chart of ASOS (over five years)

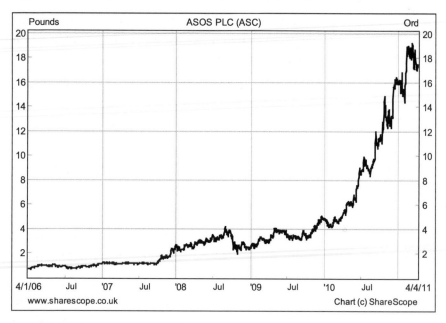

## Figure 8.4: share price chart of ASOS (over one year)

As a general rule I try never to sell when the price is rising and never buy when the price is falling. It's not an exact science and you will never get it right all the time, but that should not stop you trying.

The two key learning points from this example as far as I am concerned are:

1.  The continuing upward trend convinced me to keep at least some of my holding despite the fact that other measures were telling me to sell. That has turned out to be a great decision.

2.  If there are reasons to sell and hold you can always do both by selling part of your holding.

## Trend changes

*How do you know that a short-term change in price direction constitutes a major change in the trend itself?*

This is the million dollar question. If the price move is part of a change in trend, then it should act as a trigger for the trend trader to sell or buy; if it isn't, and it's just a short-term correction, then it should just be ignored.

You could of course just guess and place a stop or trailing stop order at what you think is an appropriate level. But it would still be a guess (even if it is an educated one), and as we have seen in the example of ASOS, it would not have worked. In such a position I would try to keep my natural emotions under control, remain disciplined and allow the moving averages (MA) to make my decision for me.

A moving average line automatically filters out all of the noise of the short-term price movements making price trends more visible. There are many different types and many ways to use them.

The MAs are calculated over different time periods, normally nine days to 200 days. Obviously, the shorter the period the more nimble and responsive it will be. Using a nautical analogy, if the nine-day MA is a speed boat then the 200-day is a tanker – the choice of which you use will largely depend on how active you want to be.

Moving averages, by their very nature, are lagging indicators as they are calculated from historical information and therefore would not be suitable for very short-term traders. For trend traders and investors, for whom this book is written, I find them a good way of deciding when a trend has changed.

With this purpose in mind I use two MAs in conjunction with each other. One over a shorter period, one longer. I personally use the 30- and 90-day options as I want them to respond to price changes, but not be over sensitive, which would lead to over-trading.

- When the shorter-term MA cuts the longer-term MA from below it is a **buy signal** as it would indicate that an uptrend may well be starting (the wider the angle as they cross, the stronger the indication). This is often referred to as a *golden cross*.

- When the shorter-term MA cuts from above it can be regarded as a **sell signal** as a downward trend may well be starting, also known as a *death cross*.

## Examples

Let's look how this works in reality. For continuity reasons I will use the same examples.

## 1. Cookson Group [CKSN]

The following graph shows the 30-day MA as a dotted line, and the 90-day MA as a dashed line. When the 30-day MA cuts through the 90-day MA from below in September 2010 it forms a golden cross and provides a buy signal.

**Figure 8.5: share price chart of Cookson Group**

## 2. ASOS [ASC]

As you can see in the following chart, the 30-day MA has remained above the 90-day so no death cross has formed yet. Therefore, I would continue to hold the residue of my holding until they do.

**Figure 8.6: share price chart of ASOS**

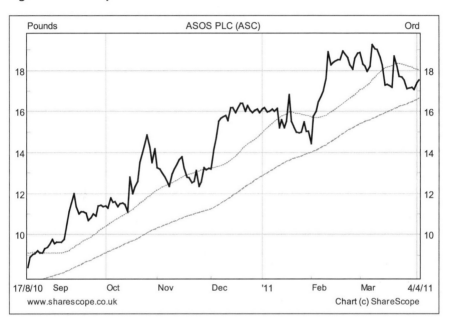

## Double tops/bottoms

One final point that you may find useful on the subject of trend changes: very often a precursor to a trend change is a *double top* or *double bottom*. This is where the price twice tries to move through a particular level, fails, and then reverses away from the level.

An example of a double bottom can be seen in the following chart:

**Figure 8.7: chart of Axis Shield [ASD] with a double bottom**

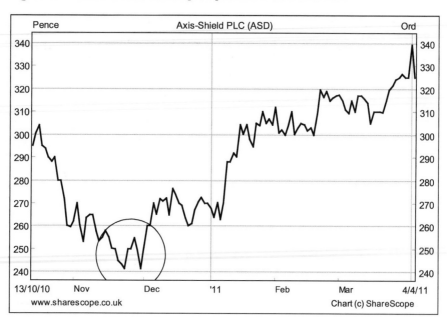

As can be seen in the chart, the price of Axis Shield had been in a downtrend when on 23rd November 2010 it closed at a low of 241.5p. The price then bounced up a little, but one week later on 30th November the price again closed at the same low of 241.5. Having twice failed to break through this level, the price then definitively reversed and rose strongly in an uptrend.

The following chart illustrates a double top:

**Figure 8.8: chart of JPMorgan American Investment Trust [JAM] with a double top**

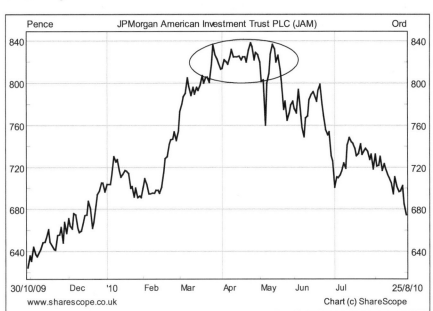

In fact, as you can see, the preceding chart actually illustrates a *triple top* – a variation of a double top, often considered to be an ever stronger indicator of a change in trend.

In summary:

• a **double bottom** is often a very *positive* sign for the price,

• a **double top** is often a *negative* sign for the price.

# History repeats itself

The idea that certain price patterns repeat themselves is a key concept in technical analysis. This suggests the market has a memory. Let's look at this in some more detail.

## Resistance

A *resistance level* is a price point at which it is thought that selling will be strong enough to prevent the price of a security from rising further. This view is informed by the price history. It is the level on a price chart at which the price previously stopped rising and began to fall and implies – to the chartist – that it will do so again.

## Support

A *support level* is the exact opposite: a price that previously brought about increased buying that resulted in a point where previously the price stopped falling and began to rise.

## Examples

Let's look at a couple of examples in which support and resistance levels worked.

Looking first at resistance levels, we will therefore be looking at the price highs. For this example we will look at shares in gas and electricity supplier Centrica [CAN].

**Figure 8.9: share price chart of Centrica (six months)**

Looking at the six-month chart you can see that four times it hit a level just above 340p and each time fell away. This is a good example of a resistance level – it just doesn't seem able to convincingly break up through that level.

Let's now look at the longer-term, five-year chart of Centrica.

**Figure 8.10: share price chart of Centrica (five years)**

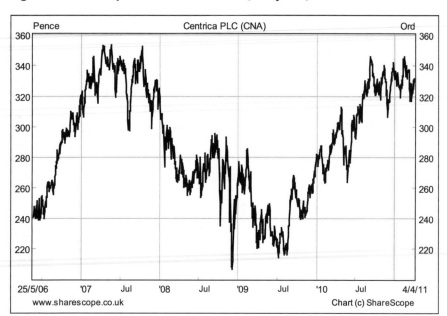

You can see that also, longer-term, the resistance level between 340 and 350 is a strong one. The more often the price rebound happens at around this level, the stronger the resistance level becomes.

Now let's turn to Barclays and an example of support levels.

**Figure 8.11: share price chart of Barclays (six months)**

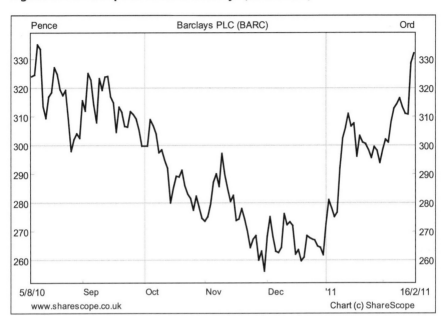

As you can see in the preceding chart, the Barclays share price was in a steady downtrend until it got to the 260p level, at which point it formed a double (or, possibly, triple) bottom and reversed trend.

*Why did it bounce off the 260p level?*

Let's look at a longer-term chart of Barclays.

## Figure 8.12: share price chart of Barclays (two year)

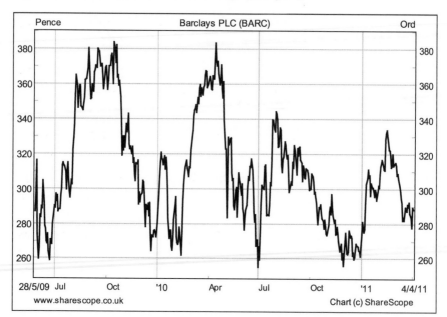

Looking at the longer-term chart of Barclays we can see that we have been here before! Several times in the previous couple of years the price has fallen to around the 260p level, failed to convincingly break through it, and then bounced up to higher levels.

History repeating itself!

Obviously, support and resistance levels do not work all the time. Nothing does. I regard them as guidelines as opposed to rigid barriers and, as such, useful more than crucial. I refer to them when setting stops and limits, but I also like to study them when I am analysing a stock. Once again my 3 Box Test passed.

# Conclusion

If technical analysis is an eight-course dinner, all I have done with this chapter is serve the hors d'oevures.

Whether technical analysis works well enough to use in isolation of other analysis is a controversial topic. Warren Buffett is among many experts who have spoken out against it, saying:

> "if past history was all there was to the game, the richest people would be librarians"

The truth is it is probably more of an art than a science, but it certainly plays a part in my investment selections. I believe an easy way of getting a feel for a stock is quickly reviewing the price charts over various time periods, from, say, five years down to one month. Each may well display different highs and lows. You may feel, like I do, that it may help you to decide which way a share may move in the future if you see where it has come from and at what price levels it previously changed direction.

I don't think that history repeats itself perfectly but – as Mark Twain said – perhaps it does rhyme, and just rhyming can be enough sometimes to be useful.

# CHAPTER 9:

## INVESTING OR TRADING?

There are two ways to make money in the stock market: you can invest or you can trade. The figures in the first chapter should have given the potential investor all the statistics he or she would ever need to justify his or her long-term participation in the stock market. The position is not quite as clear-cut for trading.

That said, I think trading is an activity that should in most cases be added to the investor's repertoire. At the very least, as I will go on to explain in this chapter, I believe that the investor today should think less in terms of just "buy and hold" and more in terms of "buy, build, reduce and sell".

## The trading investor

I see myself as 90% investor and 10% trader. Trading not only in my dealing accounts, but also on occasion in my ISA and SIPP accounts. Think about your own situation and come up with an investment/trading ratio that works for you. I would encourage even the most long-term "buy and hold" investor to consider adding an element of trading to their investment portfolio.

It's not just a question of should you invest or trade and in what proportions, but even for the 100% investor there is the question of how active should one be?

The greater level of volatility in the markets in my opinion has increased the importance of adopting a more active investment approach. Although the final destination of the stock market journey is just the same, the journey is very different. This being the case, a long-term "buy and hold" policy will still work. However, what perhaps will work better in these more volatile markets is a more active investment policy. The investor should try not to think just in black and white terms: should I buy or sell? Think also about the question: should I build or reduce a holding? This approach offers many benefits:

1.  You can **take advantage of market volatility**. By increasing holdings when prices are low and decreasing them when they are relatively high you can reduce the average acquisition cost of each unit of investment you retain.

2.   You can **reduce risk**. You are making sure you don't buy or sell completely at the wrong time.

3.   You **stop yourself becoming too attached to a holding**. Until the sale takes place the investor can hide behind the statement "you don't incur the loss until you sell". To put it another way, the whole decision to buy the stock in the first place is never wrong until the loss is crystallised. Human nature being what it is, this means that a significant number of investors only sell the holdings that are making profits and therefore end up with a portfolio of loss makers! The total reverse of what I would regard as the best policy of "running your profits and cutting your losses". By building and reducing holdings you reduce the risk of becoming too attached to an individual stock and the whole portfolio can have a far more fluid and market sensitive feel to it.

The last point is a very important one and in my opinion is one of the most common mistakes that investors make. They take the fact that a particular investment has lost money too personally. They shouldn't. As John Maynard Keynes once said, "The markets can stay irrational longer than you can remain solvent." So it's not a question of being right or wrong, it's just that the markets don't agree. Cut your losses, run your gains and move on. That's what makes risk control mechanisms that make sure you do not "put all your eggs in one basket" so important.

## The selection of instrument to trade

The term and the actual investment you are trading will best determine the vehicle you use. If you are looking to trade blue chips or indices over very short periods then you should at least consider vehicles such as Contracts for Difference or Financial Spread Trading. These and other leveraged vehicles obviously involve higher risk, but they do provide you with very effective use of capital and an exemption from stamp duty.

"Every trader should also invest, but not every investor needs to trade."

If, however, you want to trade small cap stocks or you are uncomfortable with the increased risk of leveraged investments then it is quite appropriate simply to trend or swing trade the stocks themselves. However, it has to be said, even if you opt to take the lower risk option of using the physical investment as opposed to its leveraged counterpart, trading is still a much higher risk discipline than investing. There is an obvious correlation between risk and time.

Nothing reduces the risk of the market more than time; the ability to wait for the growth. Therefore, I would say that every trader should also invest, but not every investor needs to trade.

## Volatility as a Good Thing

The stock market has always had two fundamental characteristics:

1.   long-term growth, and

2.   short-term volatility.

The case for investing is based on the former, the argument for trading on the latter. Trading is all about using the volatility to your advantage. In other words, viewing volatility – a feature of the stock market that many investors dislike – as a benefit.

Although short-term volatility has always been a feature of the stock market, I would say that volatility levels have increased greatly over the last 15 years as paper-based dealing systems have been replaced by computer-driven programs.

As volatility has increased, so have the opportunities to trade. Stocks and indices move into oversold or overbought positions on a far more frequent basis. This should be viewed by both investors and traders alike as an opportunity, not a threat – an opportunity to buy stocks or indices at a discount or sell them at a premium. It is a direct result of this increased volatility that the modern day trader has been born.

## Examples of oversold stocks

Recent examples of oversold stocks would be:

**Figure 9.1: Barclays at 51p in January 2009**

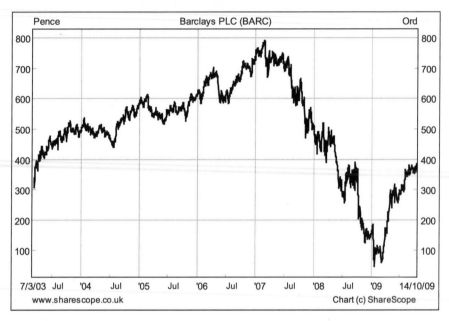

**Figure 9.2: Lloyds at 20p in March 2009**

**Figure 9.3: BP at 302p in June 2010**

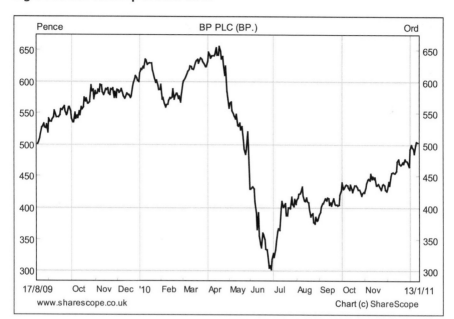

You may jump to the conclusion that you need a global bank crisis or a massive oil disaster to provoke such price reactions, but this is far from the case.

Let's take a blue chip share, in the top ten shares by market capitalisation quoted on the London markets, with a forecast yield at that time of 7% and a PE of eight. Surely this will be more stable? Well, only marginally!

AstraZeneca [AZN] is the company that fits this profile and in March 2008 this was priced at 1748p, not far short of half the price that it is today.

## Figure 9.4: AstraZeneca

Also, don't just think these opportunities apply to individual companies. The FTSE 100 itself was at 3512 as recently as March 2009.

## Figure 9.5: FTSE 100 Index

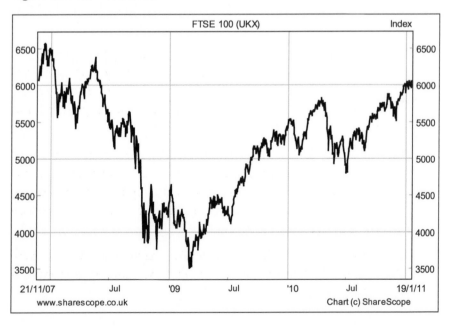

# Trading

Let's look at the most basic differences between investing and trading.

|  | Investing | Trading |
|---|---|---|
| Outlook | long-term | short-term |
| Primary focus | value | momentum |
| First reference | fundamentals | charts |
| Key question | what should I buy? | when should I sell? |

The investor's focus, therefore, should be on fundamentals such as the dividend, dividend cover, PE and PEG. The exact price they pay is of less importance than what they buy and the long-term business case. They should ask themselves: "Is this a company I would like to own?"

Trading, on the other hand, is all about the price and momentum. They need to develop a discipline to dictate not just when to buy, but even more crucially when to sell.

## Types of trader

I would define a trader as someone who makes decisions based on price and momentum with a view to making a short-term profit. However, for greater clarity I would subdivide traders into three categories:

1. A **day trader** trades within a day and rarely holds any positions open at the end of the day (i.e. in theory it means they sleep well at night with no exposure to the markets overnight). This is a specialised area and really is not within the remit of this book. However, it is good to know it exists and where it fits.

2. **Swing traders** normally use technical analysis to detect support and resistance levels and use these to inform trading decisions. Normally the trade would be opened at, or close to, the support level and closed at, or near, the resistance level. The duration of the trade would often be counted in weeks, not days.

3. **Trend traders** trade an identifiable trend in the direction of the current momentum. The trade duration can often be counted in months as opposed to weeks.

The shorter the holding period of the trade, the more likely a trader is to use leveraged instruments (e.g. CFDs). Trend traders may use leveraged instruments or the cash instrument. It is trend trading using the cash instrument (e.g. trading simple shares, and not CFDs on shares) that I want to examine here and is the category that novice traders and investors, for whom this book is written, should focus on initially.

# Trend trading

One of the main potential advantages of leveraged investments is that you can make money if the object of the trade falls in value by going short. I would stress the word "potential" because you still have to get the direction of the trade correct and I think as a general rule it is harder to get a short trade right than it is a long one for the simple reason that the markets tend to rise more than fall. Just because you can technically make money via leveraged investments when the markets rise or fall does not mean you will. However, as I am only discussing here trend trading the physical investment, we will only be considering long trades.

I regard trend trading to be the middle ground between day trading and long-term investment.

| | | longer holding time ⟶ | | |
|---|---|---|---|---|
| day trading | swing trading | trend trading | active investing | buy and hold investing |

The first three trading styles in the previous diagram are all price-focused activities. One of the main differences between the three will be the level of tolerance to price volatility when the transaction is running. As a rough rule I would expect the day trader to close a trade if it moved 2-3% against them, a swing trader to do the same at loss levels of 4-5%, but the tolerance for trend traders would be wider and should be more like 8-10%.

The object of this type of trend trade is to spot an upward trend and ride it until it changes. The sooner you can identify the trend and the longer you can ride it, the more money you will make. Because the holding period for a trend trade is normally quite short, one needs a strong methodology to time the trade well. So let's look at my way of deciding what and when you should buy.

## The perfect trend trade

My perfect trend trade of a share would have four key elements:

1.  A value marker,

2.  a catalyst for movement,

3.  limited downside, and

4.  momentum.

We'll now look at each of these elements in a bit more detail.

### 1. The value marker

By value marker I mean an indicator that would identify the share as undervalued at the current price. As already explained, I believe the PEG is the best indicator to perform this role. Normally you would associate such a fundamental measure to be more a tool for the investor than the trader. However, if a stock is undervalued, as opposed to just being cheap, I believe it will also offer greater potential upside for the short-term trader. It will tend to move quicker and further. A PEG of less than one is the value measure I look for.

### 2. The catalyst

The PEG may tell you that the shares are good value with the potential to move up, but they still require a catalyst to get things going. This could be a piece of news, a rating change by a broker, a director's purchases, or something else. My personal favourite is a director's purchase – preferably multiple deals of significant size at full market value.

### 3. Limited downside

When you trade it is best to do so with the protection of a support level close to the purchase price. In this type of trade the ideal level would be within 15-20%. By placing a stop order to sell just below the resistance level, you can help limit the potential downside risk of the trade.

## 4. Trend direction

The best tool to identify changes in trend are the price charts. The ultimate trend change to pick up on in these circumstances is when a downtrend ends and an uptrend starts. There are many measures you can use but I would recommend using the 30- and 90-day moving averages in conjunction with each other. When the 30-day moving average moves up through the 90-day moving average (the *golden cross*) you can legitimately take the view that a new uptrend has started.

## Example: Communisis

For continuity reasons I will use the one-year chart for Communisis [CMS] to illustrate this type of trade. This is one of the stocks I earlier used to demonstrate the significance of directors' purchases. It can make perfect sense to both trade and invest in the same stock at the same time because you should be more familiar with the stock. This is what I chose to do in this case, and although the *trade* has long since been closed, the *investment* remains in my portfolio. Let's complete the circle and see what happened.

The stock came to my notice first in January 2010. It appeared on the watch lists produced by my stock filters as it had a **PEG of 0.8**. The series of directors' deals (marked on the chart) acted as the **catalyst** for the trade. The **support level** about 15% below gave the desired protection and the crossing of the 30- and 90-day moving averages marked the change in trend and **momentum**. Accordingly, all four boxes for the perfect trend trade were ticked!

## Figure 9.6: Communisis

## The catalyst for the trade – directors' deals

I reproduce the following table of directors' deals for this stock that acted as a catalyst for the trade.

| Chart legend | Date | Directors' deal |
|---|---|---|
| A | 11/11/2009 | Andy Blundell – Buy 50,000 shares at 19p |
| B | 03/12/2009 | Peter Hickson – Buy 50,000 shares at 17p |
| C | 09/12/2009 | Peter Hickson – Buy 50,000 shares at 15p |
| D | 18/12/2009 | Peter Hickson – Buy 100,000 shares at 14p |
| E | 24/12/2009 | John Wells – Buy 25,000 shares at 14p |
| F | 31/12/2009 | Alistair Blaxill – Notification of Holding |
| G | 25/02/2010 | John Wells – Buy 20,000 shares at 14p<br>Peter Hickson – Buy 350,000 shares at 14p<br>Roger W Jennings – Buy 30,000 shares at 14p |
| H | 26/02/2010 | John Wells – Buy 15,000 shares at 15p<br>Michael Graham Firth – Buy 100,000 shares at 15p |

As you can see from the graph, the positive momentum continued and the price moved upwards. But a trade is only successful and complete when you take your profits. Just as you needed a plan to tell you what and when to buy, you also need to a plan to time the sale. I have two preferred options. I often use the momentum indicator in reverse. Just as the relative movement of the 30- and 90-day moving averages helped time the entrance, they can also be used to time the exit. Alternatively, you could set a target price and use a limit order to sell.

## The result

An ideal trade, which would have realised a profit of 60% over a four-month period using either of the two exit methods:

1.  **Trend change**: you would have sold when the 30-day moving average cut the 90-day line from above (the dead cross).

2.  **Target price**: working to my usual 3-to-win/1-to-lose ratio (explained in chapter 12), the stock bought at 15p would have a stop loss order for protection at 12p (3p below) and therefore the limit order to sell to take the profits would have been 9p above (3 x 3p) the purchase price at 24p.

By coincidence, in this example the exit point (determined by the change in trend indicated by the 30- and 90-day MAs) and the initially set target price set by the limit order and stop orders would have been the same.

The important point to take on board here is that when you trade you must have a plan for when to buy and when to sell. The old saying has merit:

*plan your trade and trade your plan*

Which exit strategy you use is a matter of personal choice: you could even use both, but you must have one if you are going to trade effectively.

# Investors and traders play by different rules

When it comes to comparing investment and trading I will make one last observation. The most successful investors I have met in my working life tend to be contrarian by nature and use the fundamentals as their first point of reference.

Most successful short-term traders do exactly the opposite. They move with the consensus investing in the direction of the current momentum and exit their position when this subsides or reverses; and use the charts as their first reference point.

"When you trade you must have a plan for when to buy and when to sell."

It is interesting that what tends to work best in each discipline are the exact opposites.

# CHAPTER 10:
## EXCHANGE TRADED FUNDS (ETFS)

ETFs are open-ended index funds that are traded on stock exchanges. In other words, they are tracker funds that are priced continually on the markets that you can buy and sell immediately like any share.

They are the biggest growth story of the stock market over recent years and for good reason.

## Low cost

A great attraction of ETFs is that they are cheap:

1. **Low Total Expense Ratios** (TER), which are the annual charges made by the fund; ETF TERs range from a low of 0.15% to a high of 0.85% pa.

2. There are **no front-end fees**.

3. There is **no stamp duty** charged on purchases.

4. They offer very **small bid/offer spreads**.

You could claim, therefore, they offer the best of both worlds: the diversification of a fund and the cheap and efficient tradability of a share.

# Range of ETFs

There are now almost 1000 ETFs (and ETCs) listed on the London Stock Exchange. You can find a comprehensive list of ETCs on the London Stock Exchange website (**www.londonstockexchange.com**). The range is, frankly, huge. There are ETFs that track individual markets (e.g. Korea, Turkey), ETFs on regions (e.g. East Europe, Pacific Ex-Japan), ETFs on global sectors (e.g. global water, timber and forestry), on investing styles (e.g. growth, value), as well ETFs on government and corporate bonds.

The following table shows the most actively traded ETFs on the London Stock Exchange for the first three months of 2011:

## Table 10.1: most active ETFs on LSE (Jan-Mar 2011)

|    | ETF | EPIC |
|----|-----|------|
| 1  | iShares FTSE 100 | ISF |
| 2  | iShares S&P 500 | IUSA |
| 3  | iShares MSCI Japan | IJPN |
| 4  | iShare DJ Euro STOXX 50 | EUE |
| 5  | iShares FTSE UK Div Plus | IUKD |
| 6  | db x-trackers FTSE 100 | XUKX |
| 7  | Lyxor ETF FTSE 100 | L100 |
| 8  | iShares FTSE 250 | MIDD |
| 9  | iShares FTSE UK All Stocks Gilt | IGLT |
| 10 | iShares FTSE EPRA NAREIT UK Property Fund | IUKP |
| 11 | iShares GBP Index Linked Gilt | INXG |
| 12 | iShares MSCI Emerging Markets | IEEM |
| 13 | iShares MSCI World | IWRD |
| 14 | iShares MSCI Emerging Markets | IDEM |
| 15 | MW TOPS Global Alpha ETF EUR Shares | MWTE |
| 16 | iShares MSCI World | IDWR |
| 17 | db x-trackers FTSE 100 Short ETF | XUKS |
| 18 | db x-trackers FTSE All-share ETF | XASX |
| 19 | iShares MSCI North America | IDNA |
| 20 | iShares MSCI AC Far East ex-Japan | IFFF |

### Short and leveraged ETFs

Besides ordinary ETFs, there are also ETFs described as *short* and *leveraged* (these words will appear in their name). The former are designed to appeal if you feel the underlying index will fall in price, and the latter increase the gain or loss relative to the price of the underlying (and thereby increasing risk in the same proportion). Be very careful with both – they are designed more for traders than investors. I would recommend avoiding them.

# How ETFs can be used by investors

*But in what ways could you use them to improve your investment strategy?*

Here are four different ways:

## 1. Core investment

By adding broad-based ETFs to a portfolio you can achieve instant diversification by investing in a whole index of shares in one trade.

Examples would be the iShares FTSE100 [ISF] or iShares S&P 500 [IUSA]. Investors can use these ETFs to lay a simple foundation for a diversified portfolio.

To illustrate the cost effectiveness of this type of fund:

* iShares FTSE100 [ISF] has a TER of 0.4%; and its price as I write is 603.8-604, a bid/offer spread of just ⅛th of a penny!

* iShares S&P 500 [IUSA] has the same TER of 0.4%; and is currently priced at 818.75-819.25, a bid/offer spread of just half a penny.

## 2. Trade an index

You can use ETFs to take a short-term view on an index. If I was going to trade an index without using a leveraged instrument (i.e. not using CFDs or spread betting), ETFs are the type of vehicle I would use as they are ideally suited to this purpose. They have narrow bid/offer spreads, have no stamp duty payable on purchase and have no front end fee. Also, as they are priced continuously, you can buy or sell them immediately. You can also facilitate the trade by using advanced deal mechanisms (discussed in the next chapter): you can set limits, stops and trailing stop orders using ETFs, which you can't with other funds such as unit trusts or OEICs. This means you can get on with your day job and leave the trade to work itself.

## 3. Invest on a worldwide basis

You can use ETFs to achieve global diversification – they offer a simple way of accessing overseas markets. In one trade you can invest in a market that otherwise is not easily accessible to the ordinary investor. Examples include Brazil [IBZL], Korea [IKOR] and China [FXC].

But make sure you are tracking the right index. For instance, the Chinese iShare [FXC] tracks the FTSE China 25, an index of the largest 25 Chinese shares quoted on the Hong Kong stock market. This is very different from tracking the Chinese A-share market (shares that are traded in Renminbi in mainland China).

### 4. Produce an income

Some ETFs are targeted to produce an income, which may be attractive in tax-efficient ISA or SIPP accounts. Examples would include:

- gilts: iShares FTSE UK All Stocks Gilt [IGLT]
- corporate bonds: iShares GBP Corporate Bond [SLXX]
- equities: iShares FTSE UK Dividend plus [IUKD]

# ETC hedging and credit risk

If you hold shares in the iShares FTSE100 ETF, the provider (iShares) hedges itself by holding shares in the 100 constituent companies of the FTSE100 Index. In other words, iShares hold shares in Vodafone, BP, GlaxoSmithKline etc. This is done to ensure that the value of the portfolio held by iShares does indeed track the value of the FTSE100 Index. This process of hedging is termed *full replication.*

However, not all ETFs work this way. For example, sometimes partial replication is used (where not all the constituents of an index may be held), and in other cases swaps may be used. These ETFs are designed to provide all the same benefits of the full replication ETFs; they just do it in a different way.

An example of a swap-based fund is the iShare S&P CNX Nifty India Swap [NFTY] managed by Blackrock. The swap agreement in this case is between BlackRock on the one hand, and Credit Suisse, RBS and UBS as the swap counterparties who agree to deliver the performance of the index.

A reason why an ETF may be swap-based may be because it is difficult to actually buy the physical assets; this is sometimes the case in overseas markets. ETFs that use swaps are often referred to as *synthetic,* as they are not buying the real assets of the index.

Investors should realise that there is a difference in risk between the full replication and the synthetic ETFs. In the case of the former, the ETF is backed by physical assets; in the case of synthetic ETFs, they are backed by contracts that, ultimately, rely on the credit worthiness of the swap counterparties.

Personally, I have no problem with this, but it is for each investor to consider this and decide on their own policy. If you think you may lose sleep worrying about the counterparty risk or the future ability of these companies to meet their financial responsibilities, then if I were you I would simply stick to the ETFs backed by the physical assets where this risk does not exist.

Investors should always review the term sheets (available on the providers' websites) of an ETF before buying it. For example, looking at the term sheet on the iShares website for the iShares FTSE100 ETF [ISF], one can see in the first paragraph it says:

> "The ETF invests in physical index securities."

And, in the term sheet for the iShare S&P CNX Nifty India Swap [NFTY], it says,

> "The ETF tracks the index performance through the use of over collateralised (meaning that the aggregate market value of collateral taken will exceed the overall counterparty exposure), multi-counterparty swap contracts."

And later in the term sheet it gives the names of the swap counterparties (Credit Suisse, RBS and UBS).

# Conclusion

ETFs are relatively cheap and very convenient. They appeal to many different types of investor from the cost conscious to the time-deprived to the simply lazy.

They can be used for different roles in a portfolio: they can be the diversifier, the provider of global reach, the index trading vehicle or the income producer...or even all four!

I speak to an increasing number of people who see ETFs as the Total Solution. I can see why they might think this. If stock picking is so hard (and very few professional fund managers seem able to consistently beat their index benchmark), why try? Why not simply buy a few ETFs and opt for the simple life?

I can see the logic. But such a strategy won't actually match the market, due to transaction and administration costs. I believe that individual investors do have some advantages on their side that can enable them to beat professional fund managers and also to beat index benchmarks. I like ETFs, and I use them in my own portfolios, but I don't see them as the total solution. I don't think anything is.

# CHAPTER 11:
## COMMODITIES

# The fifth asset class

In the world of asset allocation commodities are now generally regarded as the fifth asset class, after cash, bonds, shares and property. Therefore, a fully diversified portfolio should have some exposure to them.

The logic that supports this view is relatively straightforward:

1. **Portfolio diversification** – not only do commodities offer exposure to different areas of the economy, as an asset class they have historically shown little correlation to equities and bonds. Therefore, their inclusion in a portfolio can often decrease the overall portfolio risk through diversification.

2. **Inflation protection** – unlike bonds, commodities are real assets and will therefore tend to retain their value in the face of inflation. As demand for goods and services increases, prices also tend to increase, as do the price of the commodities used in their production.

3. **A finite resource** – as most commodities are physically scarce, the argument exists for a long-term upward pressure on prices provided demand remains constant. If economic growth is to resume in the developed economies and continue at present levels in emerging ones, this argument is strengthened.

Investing in commodities is an area of growing interest to the retail investor as the numbers of ways of getting direct and indirect exposure to this sector have increased.

# How to invest in commodities

If the case for some exposure to commodities in your portfolio is a relatively straightforward one, the choice of investment vehicle is less so. In broad terms you have three main options:

1.  **Direct exposure** to the chosen commodity via an Exchange Traded Commodity (ETC).

2.  **Indirect exposure** by owning shares in mining and oil companies.

3.  **Managed funds** (e.g. unit trusts and OEICs) that include natural resources investment in their remit.

We'll now look in more detail at each of these three investment approaches.

## 1. Direct exposure – Exchange Traded Commodities (ETCs)

These open-ended investment vehicles are relatively new to the retail market. They can provide you with exposure to a specific commodity or a commodity index, and trade on the markets just like a share. They have the advantage over shares of not being liable to stamp duty, but the disadvantage of not paying dividends.

### Range of ETCs

Some examples of simple ETCs on commodities are:

*   db Physical Palladium

*   ETFS Copper

*   Lyxor Gold Bullion Securities Ltd

*   UBS ETC Corn

The following chart shows the comparative price performance of Lyxor Gold Bullion Securities Ltd [GBS] and the FTSE100 Index:

## Figure 11.1: chart of Lyxor Gold Bullion Securities Ltd v. FTSE100 Index (dotted line)

As can be seen, from July 2007 gold has strongly out-performed the UK equity market; outperformance like this helps to confirm the use of such funds for diversification purposes.

ETCs also exist on commodity indices; they are designed for investors who want broad exposure to a group of commodities (e.g. agriculture, energy, precious metals) rather than exposure to individual commodities. Some examples of such index ETCs are:

- db S&P GSCI Energy

- ETFS Agriculture DJ-AIGCI

- ETFS Grains DJ-AIGCI

- Lyxor ETF CRB

Taking the ETFS Grains DJ-AIGCI as an example, this is an ETC that tracks the DJ-UBS Grains Sub-Index, which is an index that measures the aggregate prices of soybeans, corn and wheat. The following chart shows the comparative price performance of this ETFS Grains DJ-AIGCI [AGGP] and the FTSE100 Index. Use of ETCs to track diverse commodity indices like these increases the spread of the fund and therefore reduces the risk of investing in one commodity, but on occasions it has to be said it will also dilute the growth.

**Figure 11.2: chart of ETFS Grains DJ-AIGCI v. FTSE100 Index (dotted line)**

The main providers of ETCs in the UK are ETF Securities, Deutsche Bank and Lyxor, but there are a number of others. You can find a comprehensive list of ETCs on the London Stock Exchange website (**www.londonstockexchange.com**).

The following table shows the most actively traded ETCs on the London Stock Exchange for the first three months of 2011:

**Table 11.1: most active ETCs on LSE (Jan-Mar 2011)**

|    | ETC                             | EPIC |
|----|---------------------------------|------|
| 1  | ETFS Natural Gas                | NGAS |
| 2  | ETFS Leveraged Natural Gas      | LNGA |
| 3  | ETFS Corn                       | CORN |
| 4  | ETFS Wheat                      | WEAT |
| 5  | ETFS Leveraged Crude Oil        | LOIL |
| 6  | ETFS Agriculture DJ-AIGCI(SM)   | AIGA |
| 7  | ETFS Crude Oil                  | CRUD |
| 8  | ETFS All Commodities DJ-AIGCI(SM) | AIGC |
| 9  | ETFS Physical Silver            | PHAG |
| 10 | ETFS Physical Gold              | PHAU |

As with ETFs, there are also *short* and *leveraged* ETCs. As I mentioned with the ETF versions, be very careful with both – they are designed more for traders than investors. I would recommend avoiding them.

Two points I would make if you thinking of investing in ETCs:

1.  Always look at the ETC term sheets on the provider's website very carefully.

2.  Be aware of any currency risk that may be involved, as commodities are normally quoted in US$.

### ETC hedging, credit and tracking risk

Some ETCs, such as gold, silver, palladium and platinum, can be 100% backed with the physical metal held in safe custody (the clue to look for here is the word "physical" in the title). When this is the case the proposition is relatively simple, there is no credit or counterparty risk.

However, in most cases ETCs are not backed by the provider holding the physical commodity in safe custody somewhere. Instead, the provider hedges the ETC using futures or arranges a swap with an investment bank. In principle, there is nothing wrong with this, but the investor should be aware that when they buy such an ETC they are relying on the fact that nothing goes wrong with the provider's hedging arrangements.

Another side effect of hedging ETCs with futures and swaps is that, due to the costs and mechanics of managing the hedge, they can be relatively inefficient at tracking the price of the commodity.

This inefficiency is largely caused by what is called "negative roll". This is the phrase used to describe the cost incurred when the ETC provider of a non-physical fund, to avoid delivery of the commodity, has to sell one futures contract, which is nearing its expiry, to purchase another longer dated one. Very often the cost of the new one is higher than the old and this can, over the long-term, reduce the return from this type of fund.

Although it is possible to benefit from positive rolls (buying the new future at a lower price than the one sold), the reverse is more the norm. I know many investors who have been very disappointed with this feature of these non-physical funds, which can often result in the fund price significantly underperforming the spot price of the commodity in question. However, because there are few alternatives (unless you can find a place to store 1000 barrels of oil!), this may be a price that investors have to pay to get this more direct exposure in this area.

## Gold and oil

The two commodities that are by far the most popular with investors are without doubt gold and oil.

Gold tends to be regarded as a defensive commodity, one that performs best when markets struggle, while oil tends to be the reverse. However, the current behaviour of both is I am afraid far from straightforward.

Gold at the time of writing is near its all-time high at over US $1500 per ounce. A reason for its rise is its traditional safe haven status – important in the current uncertain times. Many commentators feel that the price of gold will continue to rise, and there may be something still to go for if you are trading over the short-term. However, for the longer-term investor that this book is predominantly written for, buying at near record levels is rarely the best idea.

The future price movement for oil is also hard to predict. There is no doubt that new discoveries are becoming harder to find. Logic would therefore support what is known as the *peak oil theory*. However, on the other hand, reserves have never been higher. The *Financial Times* reported on 14th September 2010 that present inventories for the developed world were showing 2800m barrels held in reserve, equating to 61 days of supply. The last time reserves were this high was in 1998 when the price was five times cheaper!

## 2. Indirect exposure – mining and oil companies

Shares in the mining and oil sectors have always been included in the main indices on the London Stock Exchange, but rarely have they had such a significant presence. At the time of writing six of the largest 20 companies on the LSE are from these sectors. In decreasing order of size these are currently:

- Shell [RDSB]
- BP [BP.]
- Rio Tinto [RIO]
- BHP Billiton [BLT]
- Anglo American [AAL]
- Xstrata [XTA]

The events surrounding BP have brought an unwanted but nevertheless timely reminder of the danger of stock-specific investment. Nevertheless, almost without exception, using PE and PEG ratios these companies would appear to be not only cheap but also undervalued.

Some may argue that they appear undervalued for a good reason – they are high risk companies in high risk sectors in a high risk market.

But, even allowing for the potential problems, I feel that value still remains for the long-term investor, and right now a diversified group of miners and oil companies would be my preferred method of gaining exposure to this area of the market.

## The leverage effect

Many believe that investment in mining companies will increase (leverage) the return you would get from investment in the commodity itself and, although it's not always the case, overall I would agree with them.

Take a gold miner as an example. If the price of gold rises, the value of the shares should reflect this increase as it will have an impact on current earnings. On the assumption that extractions costs remain stable in the short-term this increase in earnings should not only drop direct to the bottom line profit of the company but it also benefits from an element of leverage. For example, say a gold mining company has revenues of £10m and costs of £6m; its profit will be £4m. If the price of gold increases 10%, the revenues will increase by the same percentage from £10m to £11m. The profit, however, would now be £5m. So a 10% increase in the commodity price produces a 25% increase in profits. As we have already discussed in chapter 1, when profits rise, the share price will ultimately follow.

There is also another reason why an increase in the price of a commodity may produce a greater proportionate increase in the share price. The latter is not only affected by any increase in the commodity price today but will also take into account the increased expectations of future earnings. Accordingly, all things being equal, if the price of gold moves up I would expect the price of the gold mining shares to increase more.

### Example: Medusa Mining

A good example of a gold miner that I like and own is one that I have mentioned briefly before, when I was writing about simple business cases. Namely, Medusa Mining [MML]. The following chart shows a 2-year comparison of this share with an ETC that holds physical gold bullion (the ETF Securities fund, which trades under the ticker PHAU). This ETC appeared in the list of the most active ETCs quoted on the LSE shown earlier in this chapter.

## Figure 11.3: share price chart of Medusa Mining [MML] v gold [PHAU] (thin line)

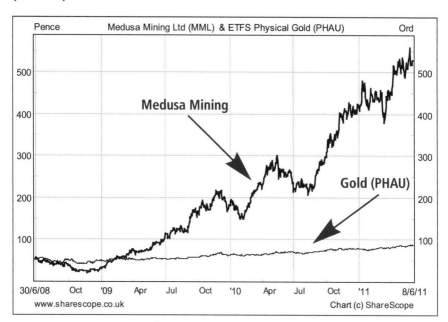

As can be seen, although PHAU (our proxy for gold) increased by 80% from the beginning of 2009 to mid 2011, that rise was eclipsed by the stellar performance of Medusa Mining, which rose 1500%! This illustrates clearly the leverage effect that can result in mining company shares magnifying the performance of the underlying commodity. Although note that this leverage effect can work both ways: in 2008 when the gold price dipped, the fall in MML shares was much greater.

### Example: Tullow Oil

Let's now compare over the same three-year period an OIL ETC (using futures) with my favoured oil explorer, Tullow Oil [TLW]. Let's take the ETC once again off the top ten traded list: CRUD. When seeking coverage of the commodity section I would prefer to focus on upstream oil companies (explorers) like this as opposed to downstream (refiners) such as Shell and BP. Obviously, there is a case for inclusion of such oil giants in your portfolio, but it is based as much on their dividend and the growth of it as much as the exploration side of their business.

**Figure 11.4: share price chart of Tullow Oil [TLW] v oil [CRUD]**

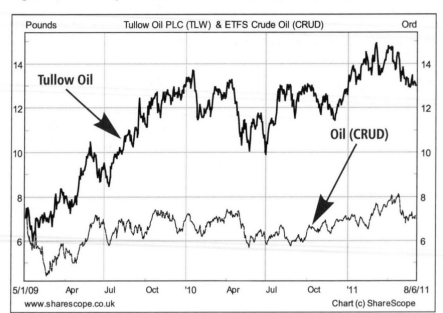

The result: a massive victory for the mining/exploration company over the underlying commodity.

You should not expect this on every occasion, but such extreme examples make the point that I want to emphasise. If you expect direct commodity investment via an ETC to make money, if you can invest in the commodity via a good mining/exploration company you can make more – sometimes a lot more!

A caveat, however. Beware the bulletin boards! No area in the market is more crowded than the mining sector and upstream oil companies with people who want to share details of the next major discovery with the world on the internet. Let the share do the talking and focus on the facts, not the rumours.

### 3. Managed funds (unit trusts and OEICs)

If you would prefer the professional management and diversification offered by a fund manager in this specialist area there are a range of funds available that focus on commodities.

One of the best things I find about managed funds is that there is such a wide choice available. But without a method to narrow your search criteria, this large choice can also be daunting. I therefore often recommend investors to use the selection tools available on the websites and, specifically, if available, use the *Financial Express* crown rating filter.

This rates funds using a three crown system based on performance over the last three years. If a fund has three crowns then it is in the top 20% of rated funds, two crowns indicates the next 30% and one crown the bottom 50%. If a fund has no rating it is because it has not been in existence for three years, or the sector is too small for meaningful comparisons to be made.

I like these ratings as they are simple and effective. They do not just measure absolute performance; I could get that from any performance league table. They also measure relative performance, risk and consistency. They pass the 3 Box Test as far as I am concerned.

There is a lot of help available on the websites, but as always if you are a self-directed investor the final choice is yours. Remember, if you use managed funds make sure you use a funds supermarket that will give you access to them at discounted rates.

# Conclusion

I think exposure to commodities is an essential part of every portfolio. How best to achieve it is a more difficult question.

The case to access indirectly via a mining or exploration company is a strong one because of the leverage effect. I have no doubts that this is the method that offers the greatest potential rewards. We should not be surprised at this, as it also involves the greatest risk.

In addition to the uncertainty of commodity prices there are additional company and geo-political risks involved that can complicate the investment. These risks and the specialist nature of the sector mean that the professional management and diversity offered by unit and investment trusts should not be dismissed lightly.

The three methods outlined in this chapter all have different merits. The greater growth potential of the individual company; the purer exposure to the commodity via a physical ETC, and the diversity; and management of a fund. A difficult choice. My preference, as already stated, is direct exposure via a diversified group of miners and upstream oil companies. As always these options are not mutually exclusive. You can do all three, and on occasions I have done so.

# CHAPTER 12:
## SMARTER WAYS TO DEAL

The simplest way to buy or sell a share is to give a *market (or, at best)* order to your broker. For example, you may tell your broker to "buy 200 shares in Diageo at market". This instructs your broker to go to the stock market immediately and buy 200 shares at whatever the current price is.

But you may not want to deal at the current price. For example, you may want to buy Diageo shares at 1100p, but the current price is 1120p. In which case, one option is to sit at your computer screen all day waiting for the price of Diageo to fall to 1100p (if it does at all), and when it does to quickly give a market order to your broker. Possible, but clumsy. A better way is to give your broker an order to buy the shares but with an upper limit of 1100p – in other words, you will only pay 1100p or less for the shares. In this case, the broker gets to watch the market closely all day and you can read a book or whatever.

The preceding is an example of an order called a *limit order*. It is one of a range of orders, collectively known as Advanced Deal Mechanisms (ADMs), that allow you to control the precise execution of an order you give to your broker in many ways. They are also sometimes called *contingent orders*, because their execution is contingent on the share price hitting or passing a pre-specified level.

This chapter looks at these contingent orders in some detail.

# The types of contingent order

## Limit orders

### Limit orders to buy

This order allows the investor to potentially buy a share at a cheaper price than currently available in the market at the time the order is placed. Should the price of the share fall to the level selected, the deal will be executed; if the share price does not fall to the specified limit level, nothing happens, no order is executed. This deal type offers investors the possibility of buying shares below the current price.

### Limit orders to sell

This order allows the investor to sell a share at a price higher than currently available in the market at the time the order is placed. Should the price of the share rise to the level selected, the deal will be executed; if the share price does not rise to the specified limit level, nothing happens; no order is executed. This deal type offers investors the possibility of selling shares at higher than the current price.

### The problems of limits

Limits orders are disparaged by some technical analysts; they will highlight the fact that limit orders to buy are always triggered from above and limit orders to sell triggered from below. This being the case, it means that you are buying a share with a falling price and selling one with a rising price, which admittedly is not ideal for the investor and normally the exact opposite of what a trader would do. And the action of limit orders would seem to go against the old stock market adage:

*run your profits and cut your losses.*

Although I appreciate this view, I think that limit orders can still be valuable tools for both the investor and trader.

Although I would always try to avoid buying or selling against the existing trend, limits have a part to play in the management of my portfolio. I am perfectly happy for these two contradictory beliefs to co-exist in my mind.

When the share moves within a trading range, limit orders work perfectly well. The fact is that more often than not shares *will* trade within a range. When a share breaks out of the range you can always change your position. Limit orders often help me to buy lower and sell higher, and whether I am investing or trading that has got be a good thing.

## Stop orders

### Stop orders to buy

This type of order is like a market (at best) order to buy, but the order is only activated when the share price hits a specified level (that is *above* the current price).

This order is the least used of all the advanced order types, probably because it is counter-intuitive to buy shares at a higher level than the current price. And it does sound odd at first. However, the order can be useful for those whose trading decisions are driven partly by charts. By placing the contingent order just above, say, a resistance level, investors aim to buy a share with upward momentum just after it has broken through the previous resistance barrier.

Let's look at an example:

**Figure 12.1: share price chart of Morgan Crucible Company**

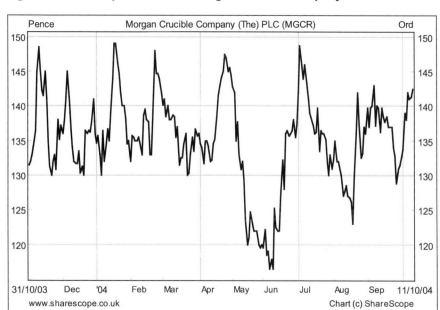

As you can see, for about a year the share price of Morgan Crucible traded in a sideways range – generally bouncing between 130p and 150p, with a brief dip down below 120p. An investor might have liked the company for fundamental reasons, but was reluctant to make an investment while the share price was stuck in such a tight range. They might have believed that if the share price could convincingly break through the 150p level, then the shares would rise much higher. As such, they would be happy to buy the shares at 155p when, and if, they ever reached that level, but not before.

*But when might this happen?*

A solution for this investor would be to place an order to *buy the shares with a stop at 155p.*

Let's see what would have happened next:

**Figure 12.2: share price chart of Morgan Crucible Company**

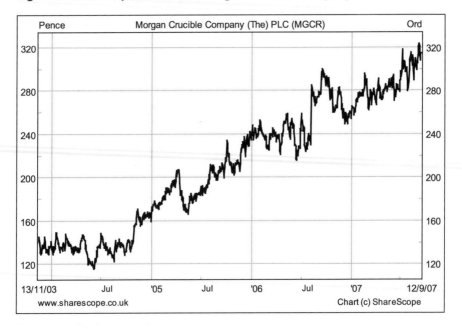

We can see that in October 2004 the shares did finally break out of the range, and rise steadily thereafter (as anticipated by the investor). When the shares hit 155p (the level of the stop), the investor's order would have been activated and his broker would then have bought the shares at market.

The advantage of such an order is that it allows the investor to set the terms of his entry into a share, which hopefully buys into future momentum. They can then get on with their day jobs and leave the broker to get on with theirs and execute the deal on their behalf as and when the share breaks through its resistance level.

## Stop orders to sell

As before, this type of order is like a market (at best) order to sell, but the order is only activated when the share price hits a specified level (that is *below* the current price). These orders are often referred to as *stop loss* orders.

This is the most used of all the advanced order types. It is used by both investors and traders to protect existing gains or to limit potential future losses.

## Comparing limit and stop orders

Investors sometimes get confused about the difference between limit and stop orders and where to put the specified levels – the table summarises this:

|  | Position of specified level to current share price |
|---|---|
| Limit order to buy | below |
| Limit order to sell | above |
| Stop order to buy | above |
| Stop order to sell | below |

For example, if the current share price is 50p:

- a **limit order to buy** would set the limit somewhere *below* 50p.

- a **stop order to buy** would set the stop somewhere *above* 50p.

### Trailing stop order to sell

For me, this is the most important and effective of all the advanced orders. It is a dynamic order that tracks a share price during the order period and sells when the price falls by a pre-determined amount from the recent high. Every time the price of a share hits a new high, the order automatically sets a new sell level. It behaves like a ratchet. The sell price will follow the current price at the distance to market you set in an upwards direction, but will never move down.

I just wish it had been available back in the mid 1990s when I bought a share called Shield Diagnostics (now called Axis-Shield).

It was late 1995 and the share price of this small medical diagnostic company was 130p and I purchased 5000 shares. From the date of purchase the shares rose from £1.30 to over £11.30. What an easy game this investing appeared back then during the dot-com boom!

Although not a web-based company, the dot-com crash was as much about how small "jam tomorrow" companies were valued, and this was such a company. You can see what subsequently happened to the price on the following chart. During the next five years I watched the share price rise about 1000%; and then in the following two years I watched it fall all the way back to where it started. All I did was watch it go up and watch it go down again.

Not clever!

I suppose it's easily done when a share price has started to fall and you have missed the peak. You tell yourself if it ever got back to £11.30 you would sell it like a shot – but of course it never did. Even if it had, the truth is you would probably hang on for £12!

**Figure 12.3: share price chart of Axis-Shield – I rode it up and all the way down**

In a long-term investment situation like this you can use the trailing stop order to protect the gain you have already made. I just wish they existed back then!

The market rarely moves in a straight line, and as you will see from the preceding chart the share price had two upward surges. One in the first half of 1997 and the other right at the end of the dot-com boom in late 1999 and early 2000. In between these growth periods the price fell back from about £7.50 to about £3.70. If a trailing stop order had been in place, then I would have undoubtedly set it at a level that would have sold my holding during this period. As this was a long-term investment I would probably have set the distance to market at between 10%-15% and at the time this would have translated to somewhere between 75p and 100p. This would have meant that I would have been taken out of the position by a trailing stop order at around the £6.50 mark. Not perfect in view of the fact the share did rise to £11.30, but better than watching all the gain disappear!

As shown previously, this type of order can be used by investors to run a profit on a holding yet protect the position at the same time. And it can also be used by traders who want to sell when a trend changes.

### Stops tighten as price increases

This type of order is expressed in pence, not as a percentage. This means as the price rises, the trailing band tightens and therefore the level of protection increases. This makes perfect sense to me. As the price rises, so does the potential capital gain on the shares. The greater the value to protect, the higher the level of protection you should seek.

Take, for example, a trailing stop order for a share priced at £2. If you set your trailing stop to sell with a trailing band of 50p this would be 25% below the current price. However, if the share price rises to £5, the trailing stop is still 50p below the current price (i.e. at £4.50); but at this level the trailing stop is just 10% below the current price. I like this automatic feature. As the share price increases, especially if I feel it's getting toppy, the tighter I want my spreads.

I think the trailing stop order to sell is the best and most underused type of advanced orders.

At a recent investment seminar at which I was speaking, I took the opportunity of introducing a couple of clients to each other. Both were well known to me and superficially they had very similar financial profiles: both were retired in their 60s and very successful and knowledgeable long-term investors. I thought they would share ideas and get on well. However, despite the fact they had both been successful in the stockmarket over a long period they didn't seem to agree on anything! But it's worth mentioning the one thing they were 100% in agreement on was that they should have used trailing stop orders far more than they had to protect existing gains! The automatic tightening of the protection as the price rose was the feature they both liked most. When two successful investors agree they have made the same mistake I think you should sit up and take notice.

## Trailing stop orders to buy

These orders are used often by trend traders or investors hoping to buy shares cheaply after they have bottomed out and began an upward trend. If the weakness of limit orders to buy is seen to be they buy a stock that is falling, and the weakness of stop orders to buy is that they buy at a price that is higher than the current one, then a trailing stop order is seen by some to be a solution. I am not so certain. The problem here is that you have no idea at what price the deal will be executed, so setting a distance to market that fits a future unknown scenario is very difficult.

It's not that the thinking is completely flawed; I just believe there are better ways to bottom fish and trend trade. I think that for both objectives it can be a step too far for an automated order. If I am bottom fishing for a share, I want to be informed both by the fundamentals and the charts. It's true, ideally, I would want to see a reversal of the downward trend, but I would like to see the chart to be able to estimate how much I want the share price to move up from its low price. I believe these types of transactions in these circumstances often lend themselves to manual as opposed to automated orders. I would only use a trailing stop order to buy over a short period if I knew I was tied up doing something else and would not have the time to keep the position under review.

I see the role of ADMs in trend trading more as a method of managing the trade once it's up and running as opposed to timing the original entrance.

## The problem of spikes

Very often investors will complain to me about being spiked out when they use stop orders. I will discuss the levels at which you should set your orders later as this is important. However, whatever you do to alleviate the problem you cannot entirely remove it.

I am afraid when you use these stop orders, getting spiked out from time to time is a fact of life in the stock market. If you don't like this, don't use them.

# The benefits of Advanced Deal Mechanisms

## 1. No extra charge

Despite the fact that each type of order adds value, they cost the same as a normal "quote and deal" order. In addition, if the price condition set is not met then no deal is done and no charge is made. A form of price insurance, but with no premium to be paid.

## 2 Convenience

They allow you to manage your investments even when you are not in a position to monitor them. Many investors use these orders for peace of mind when they are away from the market on holiday or busy at work.

## 3. Remove the emotion from the dealing process

It's often said that there are only two things that really drive the markets: fear and greed. While I will always believe the fundamentals will re-assert themselves in the longer-term, there is no doubt that these two emotions play a major part in the determination of short-term price levels. It's so easy to find yourself caught up in the action of the price, such that you can end up executing deals in haste that you repent at your leisure...or, as in the case of Axis Shield, waiting for the share to hit a new peak before you sell. This makes no sense, waiting for an extra £1 on the price but risking (and losing) £8 in the process! Advanced dealing mechanisms help you to plan your entrances and exits beforehand, and make calculated decisions away from the frenzy of the market when it is open. In short, advanced dealing mechanisms add discipline to your buying and selling.

# Trading with ADMs

Having placed an order that is designed to limit your downside risk (such as a stop loss order) you need to put in place a profit-taking mechanism.

On a trend trade I always start with a ratio of 3:1. This means that if the stop loss is designed to cut losses at 10%, profits should be taken at three times this figure (i.e. 30%). Do this by placing a limit order to sell 30% above the original buy price. This way all things being equal you will make 30% on a successful trade and lose 10% on an unproductive one. This ratio and plan makes sense to me as it means that if I get 50% of my original investment decisions wrong I will still double my money as I will make three times as much on a winner as I will lose on a failed trade.

This plan is implemented after opening a position in a share by simultaneously placing two contingent orders:

1.  a **stop loss** order to sell *below* the current price, *and*

2.  a **limit** order to sell *above* the current.

(This is the strategy I used trend trading Communisis, detailed in an earlier chapter.)

> "It means that if I get 50% of my original investment decisions wrong I will still double my money."

After having placed these orders, if you then become more bullish on the share (perhaps as it approaches your limit to sell), you have the option of cancelling both orders and replacing with a trailing stop order to sell. This will result in letting your profits run, rather than cutting the profit at the level of the previous order limit.

## Example

Referring to the following diagram, if the original purchase was at 100p and the support level was at 95p (that I determined by looking at the chart), I would have placed a stop order to sell at 90p. The limit order to sell, using a 3:1 ratio, would have been at 130p.

**Figure 12.4: diagram of a trade using ADMs**

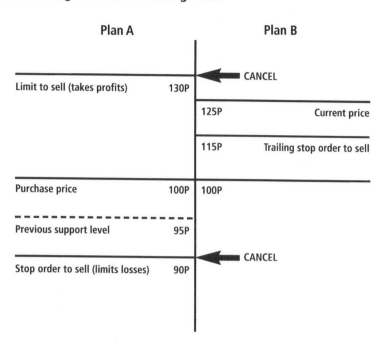

If, when the price was at 125p, you still liked the share, then you could implement plan B. To do this, you would cancel the existing stop and limit orders, and place a trailing stop order at, say, 10p below the current price (which would initially trigger if the share price fell to 115p). This may mean if the share price then falls you may make only 15% instead of the planned 30% on the trade, but it also means that if the share price continues to rise you can run with your gains trailing the share price 10p behind.

I often use trailing stop orders in this way.

# What level do you set for limit and stop orders?

A very common question with limit, stop and trailing stop orders is where to set the level for the limit or stop. In some cases, it is relatively easy, not so in others.

## Limits

The position with regard to limits is different to stops and trailing stops. Limits are used either to try to buy at a discount or sell at a premium to the current price of the security. This being the case, the level you place them will be dictated by the specific situation.

If you are trend trading using a 3:1 profit/risk ratio (as explained earlier in this chapter), then the level of the limit to sell (the point you set to take your profits) is the result of a simple mathematical calculation that would be three times the downside risk (i.e. purchase price – level of stop loss).

If you are looking to buy at a discount within a trading range it will be dictated largely by the level of the support level; the order would normally be placed just above support level.

If you are looking to sell at a premium, then again it will be informed by the charts, but this time by reference to the resistance level, and the same rules apply in reverse.

## Stops

The positioning of stops to sell is far more problematical and has been the subject of hundreds of conversations I have had with investors over the years. The basic answer to the question is quite simple: place the stops close enough to the current price to provide you with the protection you are seeking, but not too close so you are taken out of the trade by normal daily volatility earlier than you would like.

*Admittedly, easier to say than to achieve!*

Of course, much depends on the term and nature of the specific trade. The shorter and more leveraged the trade, the greater protection you will need. As you move through the trading timescales, from day trade, to swing trade, to trend trade, to investment, the distance of your stops from the price should naturally widen (this book is written primarily for the investor and trend trader, but shorter-term transactions have to be mentioned sometimes to put the subject into the correct context).

Sometimes I find it can help starting out with the logical answer and working backwards. On the basis that a short-term trade is all about the price and a long-term investment is more about the company, it can help giving the stop loss level you select a reality check. The following figures seem to me reasonable levels that fit well with the anticipated duration of the transactions:

- **2%** below the current price for the *day trader*

- **4%** below the current price for the *swing trader*

- **8%** below the current price for the *trend trader*

- **15%** below the current price for the *investor*

You may regard this broad brush approach as too simplistic, which it probably is. Needless to say, these figures do need to be checked by reference to the charts and the previous volatility levels of the security in question. Nevertheless, I like simple things. At the very least it will give you a yardstick against which you can check the stop levels you select yourself. I think this makes sense as the more you like a share, the more it should be an investment based on the long-term business case as opposed to a shorter-term trade based on the current price. With an investment you should be more tolerant to price moves against you.

## 2. For the mathematician: Average True Range (ATR)

For those who regard setting the correct stop levels should be more of a science than an art, you can adopt a more sophisticated approach using the Average True Range (ATR).

This was first popularised by J. Welles Wilder in the world of commodities, but it is equally suited to equities. This is calculated by taking the aggregate of the difference between the high price and low price of a security over a number of consecutive trading days. The standard approach is to take 14 days, but to make the arithmetic that much easier I like to use ten. You get the ATR by adding the total number of days trading range together and then dividing by the number of days the sample has been taken over. These figures are available on all the main websites under the price history of a stock; as an example, the relevant page on the Barclays Stockbrokers website is shown.

## Figure 12.5: web page showing ATR

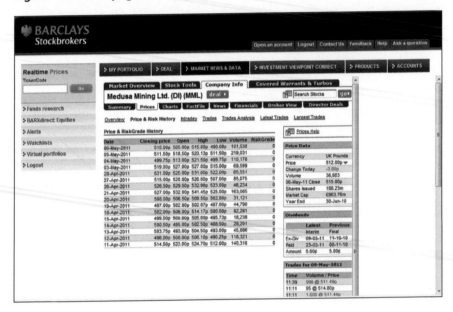

For a simple example let's take share A and imagine it moved from its intraday low to its intraday high over five of the days in question by 20p and the other five days by 10p. The aggregate range would be 150. You then divide the total by ten, making the ATR of share A 15p.

$$ATR = ((5 \times 20) + (5 \times 10))/10 = 15$$

Using the real life, previous example of Medusa Mining, taking the last ten consecutive days, the difference between the daily high and low prices were as follows (working backwards):

15, 7, 16, 9, 13, 9, 12, 22, 12, 25

These aggregate to 140, which dividing by ten (being the number of days) gives us an ATR of 14. So:

$$(15 + 7 + 16 + 9 + 13 + 9 + 12 + 22 + 12 + 25)/10 = 14$$

Once you have calculated the ATR you can use it to calculate your stop by using the following multiples:

| Trader type | % of ATR |
|---|---|
| day trader | 50 |
| swing trader | 100 |
| trend trader | 200 |
| Investor | 400 |

For illustrative purposes I have selected three shares with different recent performances. One, ASOS [ASC], has been volatile recently with fears of overvaluation driving the price down and rumours of a takeover driving it up. The other two in recent months have been more stable: Medusa Mining [MML] has risen, the other, Barclays [BARC], has been flat, In ten minutes I was able to calculate the ATR for each.

| Company | ATR |
|---|---|
| ASOS [ASC] | 77 |
| Medusa Mining [MML] | 14 |
| Barclays [BARC] | 8 |

Using this technique, if you were trend trading MML I would start (all other things being equal) with a stop 28p (ATR 14 x 200%) below the purchase price; and if I was investing in Barclays I would use a stop 32p (ATR 8 X 400%) below the purchase price.

The levels for trailing stop orders to sell should start at the same levels as their static counterparts. The significant advantage the trailing variety would add is that every time the price rises, so does the stop, locking in more of the gain, which is what this subject is all about.

Remember, when it comes to setting the level of stop losses there is no one right way to do it. All of the preceding information should help your decision-making process, but the most important

"The most important attribute to use is common sense."

attribute to use is common sense. I actually use all these factors in conjunction with each other to come to my decision. If I had to use just one, then I would use the ATR. Even then I would insist on giving the decision a final reality check by comparing them to the fixed levels outlined in the first option and use previous support and resistance levels to further inform my decision.

# Disadvantages of stops orders

## Price gaps

A disadvantage of stops is that there is not always a guarantee at what price the order will be executed at (NB. We are talking about the stock market here; the situation can be different with spread betting, where some brokers do offer guaranteed stop losses).

A market gap happens when a price jumps up or down from one level to another without passing through all the intermediate price points.

If your stop order sits within the gap it cannot be executed at the price you requested and therefore the deal may be done on far less favourable terms than you expected. Bad news such as profit warnings are rarely announced when the market is open and the opening price the following day can be very different from the closing price the night before. It can also happen when the markets are open with sudden news affecting market prices.

An example of a price gap is illustrated in the following chart of BP (during the Gulf of Mexico oil spill crisis):

**Figure 12.6: chart of BP, example of a price gap**

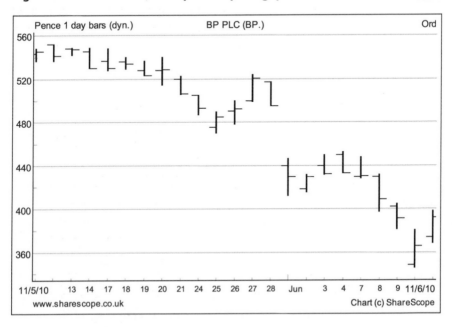

On Friday 28th May 2010, BP shares closed at 494.8p. On the following day, Saturday 29th May, BP announced that the top kill manoeuvre, started three days earlier to plug the well, had failed. Bad news. When the markets next opened, on Monday 1st June, BP shares opened at 440p (12% below the close the previous Friday). If, for example, an investor had placed a stop loss on his BP holding with the stop at 480p, on the Monday his order would have been executed at 440p (or possibly below).

## Stop limit orders

You *can* protect yourself against this to some degree by adding a limit to the price at which you are willing to deal.

For example, it is possible to place a *stop limit order*. In this case, the investor could have placed a stop order with stop at 480p (as previously), but also with a limit at 470p. This means that when the order was activated (by the pricing falling through the stop level at 480p), the order does not become a market order (thereby being dealt at whatever is the prevailing price in the market), but rather the order becomes a limit order with a limit at 470p. In this case, the order would not have been activated (because it was not possible to sell the shares at 470p or better), so nothing would have been done.

It's not easy: sometimes you want to protect yourself from being taken out of a share due to, say, an unusual price spike, other times you really do want to get out quickly at (almost) any price.

An example of placing a stop limit order is illustrated next:

**Figure 12.7: screenshot of Barclays Stockbrokers order page**

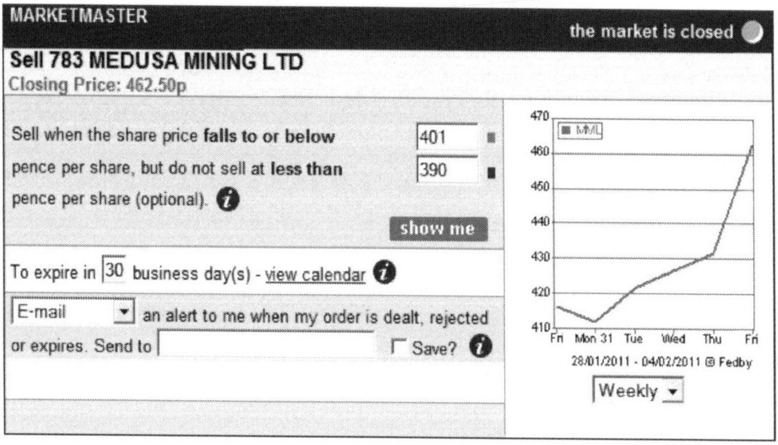

In this case, the investor is placing a stop limit order with a stop at 401p, but with a limit at 390p. So, if the shares fall to 401p, the investor wants to sell Medusa Mining shares, but not to sell them at a price below 390p.

## Guaranteed stop losses

With some stock brokers it *is* possible pay extra for guaranteed stop losses, which will execute at the price selected even if the market gaps.

*My view on both of these options?*

Unless I was dealing in leveraged investments I would ignore them both. Vehicles like CFDs and FSTs carry much greater risk; how much greater depends upon the level of gearing. This greater risk in my opinion makes stop orders a must and guaranteed stops a worthwhile investment. However, when it comes to the trend trader or investor in physical shares, I would ignore the guaranteed option. By trying to take away all the risk, or reduce it significantly, you will simply dilute the gains through extra costs. Although it may pay to do so in isolated cases, I do not think it is a good idea in the long run.

## A problem of over-trading

It's very easy, especially for people who are new to ADMs, to overuse them and to end up over-trading. This can become expensive. Never forget the cost of dealing: there's the bid/offer spread, the brokerage charges and the stamp duty on purchase. Those costs mount up.

Some traders can get hit by what are called whipsaw losses – this describes what happens when a market is largely directionless and random price movements can trigger contingent orders.

My advice is don't try to catch every twist and turn on your journey, just the major turning points. Unless you are using leveraged vehicles, don't use guaranteed stops or stops with limits; and when you are not certain at what level you should set your stop, go wider not narrower!

# My own ADM experience

I thought it would be helpful if I went back over my dealing records to see if my past experience could enlighten readers. Over the last three years I have dealt an average of eight times per month, approximately 100 times a year. Of these, 15% were dealt using ADMs. This is a lower percentage than I expected and I think it reflects my investor/trader profile. As I have already pointed out, I am 90% an investor and 10% a trend trader, and ADMs are more of a trader's tool.

From this review I find that I have used them in four specific ways:

1.   11 have been **limit orders to buy just above a support level below**. They have all been for long-term investments that I have been able to buy at a cheaper price than that prevailing when the order was placed. I only follow this policy when I am looking to buy value investments (low PE, low PEG and normally high dividend), not growth stocks. The risk of this type of deal is twofold:

    1.   You have purchased the share in a downward trend and there is a danger the share price will continue to fall after you have bought it. I find this risk is far less when buying a value share, when the price to a degree will be supported by the fundamentals. The last two shares transactions in which I have used this method were for additional purchases of AstraZeneca [AZN] and GlaxoSmithKline [GSK], both of which had forecast dividends at the time of over 5.2%. For this type of mature value share, limit orders tend to work well. I would not tend to use them for growth shares.

    2.   You don't buy the share as it does not fall to the price you have selected (and it's worse if it then proceeds to double!).

2.   Five **limit orders to sell**. Two were volatile stocks that I had thought had run their course and I wanted to try to sell on an upward spike of the market. Three were trend trades in which the limit was in place to take profits.

3.   14 **stop orders to sell** all of which were trend trades sold at a loss.

4.   15 were **trailing stop orders to sell** that replaced previous limit orders to sell as a part of a trend trade. All of these were sold at a profit.

Obviously, there were other orders that did not trigger as the price condition was not met, but I have not kept a record of these.

The weaknesses I have highlighted clearly underline the potential pitfalls in these types of orders. However, the discipline they encourage in your trading strategy is worthwhile in its own right.

*Despite the obvious imperfections in ADMs, am I glad that I use them?*

Absolutely, yes.

# CHAPTER 13:

## MY TOP TIPS FOR LONG-TERM INVESTORS

## 1. Get online

I was a total technophobe 12 years ago and made my first online trade only 11 years ago. Now, I would never deal any other way. The world has changed. If you don't want to invest online, then I would recommend you pay someone else to manage your investments or else simply buy some ETFs and track the markets. If you are not online, I don't think self-management is a realistic option.

## 2. Feed money in

For the long-term investor this is a brilliantly simple and effective way of reducing risk. Much of the risk in the stock market is short-term. Feeding money in over time, and not investing in one large lump sum, means you remove much of the risk of getting your short-term timing wrong.

## 3. Build and reduce

Don't just think in terms of buy, hold or sell; use the short-term volatility of the markets to build or reduce existing holdings. This way you can manage down the acquisition cost of your investments.

## 4. The PEG is king

When it comes to stock selection, the PEG rules. Applying the GARP system to the PEG is a simple and effective way of using the PEG as a stock selection tool.

## 5. Directors' deals

Another great stock selection tool. Look out for big value deals, small cap companies and a number of different directors buying at full market value. When they do, make sure you do as well.

## 6. Diversification

Follow the 10/2/20 Rule. In your investment portfolio don't put more than 10% in any one stock, no more than 2 shares in any one sector, but don't over dilute the portfolio by having more than 20 different holdings.

## 7. Following the dividends

Never forget the overall contribution that dividends make to the long-term return of your portfolio. When you focus on the dividend always check the cover to confirm how secure the present dividend payment is. Also watch out for those small companies who announce their maiden dividend. Very often this first dividend is seen as a vote of confidence in the immediate future of a company, and its price can react accordingly not just on the day of the announcement but for months afterwards.

## 8. Use a balance sheet

To check your progress each year do what a company does. Prepare a balance sheet. Make it simple and divide it between the different asset classes referred to in the chapter on diversification. This way you can check your wealth and diversification levels at the same time.

## 9. Maximise your tax efficiency

Invest as much as you can each year in ISAs and SIPPs. This fits in well with the recommendation to feed money into the markets, as the annual allowances will make you do this.

## 10. Don't swim against the tide!

Try never to invest against the direction of the current trend. In other words, don't buy when the price is falling and sell when the price is rising.

## 11. Sit on your hands

When you are uncertain whether to buy or sell, don't do either! There is a tendency to over-trade, often caused by a need to be doing something.

Investment is a long-term discipline and sometimes nothing is the right thing to be doing! Warren Buffett once described his investment style as, "lethargy bordering on sloth".

## 12. Keep your investment brain switched on

Keep alert for investment opportunities in your normal life: when you are shopping, when you are travelling, in your house or on holiday.

## 13. Be choosy when it comes to the company you own!

Always remember that when you buy shares you become a co-owner of the business. Do what you would do if you were buying a company in its entirety. Invest in what you know and understand.

## 14. Follow the Rule of 20

Follow a dynamic asset allocation strategy and move money round each asset class to find value. Use the Rule of 20 to guide the current proportion of your wealth you hold in shares. Add the one year forward PE of the market to the current rate of inflation. If the answer is less than 20, increase your equity investments; if it's more than 20, decrease them.

# APPENDICES

# PES AND PEGS OF FTSE100 COMPANIES

The following table lists the historic PE, forecast PE and forecast PEG for the 100 companies in the FTSE 100 Index. The companies have been ranked by PE. Note that these figures will obviously change over time (in fact they will change every time the share price moves) and so are included here only for illustrative purposes.

A few observations on the table:

1. Generally, companies at the top of the table are those where profits are expected to grow quickly (i.e. investors have bid up the share price resulting in a high PE). So, for example, technology and exploration companies can often be found near the top of the table with high PEs.

2. Generally, companies at the bottom of the table are those where profits are *not* expected to grow quickly (i.e. investors will only pay a modest price for these shares, resulting in modest PEs). Expect to find utilities and life insurance companies near the bottom of the table.

3. Companies can have atypical PE values sometimes in cases where their profits have been unusually high or low.

4. Professional investors spend much time, in effect, looking for companies that they think are in the wrong position in this table (i.e. they believe the market is pricing the shares wrongly).

5. Note how forecast PEs are generally lower than current PEs. This is because forecast profits for next year are expected to be higher than profits for this year for most companies, although not in all cases (e.g. Vodafone and Standard Life).

6. Four companies (e.g. BP) have no historic PE values. This is because those companies declared no profit (i.e. they made a loss) in the last reported accounts.

| Company Name | Sector | Historic PE | Forecast PE | Forecast PEG |
|---|---|---|---|---|
| ARM Holdings | Semiconductors | 88.0 | 54.4 | 2.0 |
| Tullow Oil | Exploration & Production | 85.9 | 18.3 | 82.2 |
| Randgold Resources Ltd | Gold Mining | 82.4 | 22.4 | 0.9 |
| Glencore International | General Mining | 58.2 | | |
| HSBC Holdings | Banks | 56.8 | 11.2 | 0.5 |
| Royal Bank of Scotland Group (The) | Banks | 46.7 | 21.4 | 0.2 |
| Hargreaves Lansdown | Asset Managers | 45.4 | 31.3 | 1.4 |
| Essar Energy | Renewable Energy Equipment | 41.1 | | |
| Burberry Group | Clothing & Accessories | 34.6 | 23.2 | 1.1 |
| Lonmin | Platinum & Precious Metals | 33.8 | 24.7 | |
| Wolseley | Industrial Suppliers | 32.7 | 15.0 | 0.5 |
| Autonomy Corporation | Software | 31.2 | 25.2 | 1.2 |
| British Sky Broadcasting Group | Broadcasting & Entertainment | 30.2 | 21.3 | 1.0 |
| John Wood Group | Oil Equipment & Services | 28.2 | 25.5 | 0.7 |
| Land Securities Group | Industrial & Office REITs | 26.5 | 23.8 | 2.3 |
| Hammerson | Retail REITs | 26.1 | 23.5 | 13.1 |
| Shire | Pharmaceuticals | 25.3 | 18.8 | 1.5 |
| British Land Co | Retail REITs | 25.0 | 19.6 | |
| Aggreko | Business Support Services | 24.8 | 23.4 | 2.6 |
| Admiral Group | Insurance Brokers | 24.2 | 20.2 | 2.1 |
| Fresnillo | Platinum & Precious Metals | 23.9 | 18.0 | |
| Intertek Group | Business Support Services | 23.6 | 18.6 | 1.1 |

| | | | | |
|---|---|---|---|---|
| Lloyds Banking Group | Banks | 22.8 | 26.1 | 0.1 |
| Johnson Matthey | Specialty Chemicals | 22.4 | 15.5 | 1.7 |
| SABMiller | Brewers | 22.1 | 17.4 | 1.5 |
| Rolls-Royce Group | Aerospace | 22.0 | 14.1 | 1.2 |
| GlaxoSmithKline | Pharmaceuticals | 21.7 | 12.0 | 1.0 |
| Weir Group | Industrial Machinery | 21.6 | 17.0 | 2.0 |
| InterContinental Hotels Group | Hotels | 20.4 | 17.8 | 1.1 |
| Capita Group (The) | Business Support Services | 19.9 | 15.0 | 1.5 |
| G4S | Business Support Services | 19.6 | 12.5 | 1.1 |
| AMEC | Oil Equipment & Services | 19.5 | 16.0 | 1.2 |
| Petrofac Ltd | Oil Equipment & Services | 19.2 | 17.3 | 1.3 |
| Antofagasta | General Mining | 18.7 | 10.4 | 8.5 |
| Diageo | Distillers & Vintners | 18.5 | 16.3 | 1.6 |
| Experian | Business Support Services | 18.5 | 16.1 | 1.4 |
| BG Group | Integrated Oil & Gas | 18.3 | 16.1 | 1.3 |
| Serco Group | Business Support Services | 18.1 | 15.5 | 1.0 |
| Pearson | Publishing | 17.1 | 14.9 | 2.7 |
| Reed Elsevier | Publishing | 16.9 | 11.9 | 1.2 |
| Sage Group (The) | Software | 16.9 | 14.7 | 2.1 |
| Compass Group | Restaurants & Bars | 16.9 | 15.4 | 1.4 |
| Inmarsat | Mobile Telecommunications | 16.3 | 12.1 | |
| Old Mutual | Life Insurance | 16.1 | 9.5 | 6.4 |
| IMI | Industrial Machinery | 15.8 | 13.2 | 1.1 |
| BHP Billiton | General Mining | 15.7 | 9.2 | 0.6 |
| Reckitt Benckiser Group | Non-durable Household Products | 15.7 | 14.5 | 14.6 |

| Associated British Foods | Food Products | 15.6 | 14.2 | 1.1 |
|---|---|---|---|---|
| British American Tobacco | Tobacco | 15.6 | 14.5 | 1.5 |
| ICAP | Investment Services | 15.5 | 11.5 | 1.1 |
| WPP Group | Media Agencies | 15.0 | 11.7 | 1.1 |
| Vedanta Resources | General Mining | 15.0 | 6.7 | 0.2 |
| Unilever | Food Products | 14.7 | 15.0 | 1.6 |
| Tesco | Food Retailers & Wholesalers | 14.7 | 11.2 | 1.0 |
| Carnival | Recreational Services | 14.6 | 14.1 | 0.7 |
| International Power | Multiutilities | 14.6 | 12.7 | 0.8 |
| Schroders | Asset Managers | 14.5 | 12.8 | 1.0 |
| Smiths Group | Diversified Industrials | 14.4 | 12.8 | 1.4 |
| Smith & Nephew | Medical Equipment | 14.3 | 14.0 | 1.5 |
| Man Group | Asset Managers | 14.2 | 12.1 | 0.3 |
| 3i Group | Specialty Finance | 13.9 | | |
| Rexam | Containers & Packaging | 13.7 | 11.4 | 1.4 |
| Imperial Tobacco Group | Tobacco | 13.5 | 10.9 | 1.3 |
| RSA Insurance Group | Full Line Insurance | 13.5 | 10.2 | 3.7 |
| Standard Chartered | Banks | 12.9 | 12.6 | 0.9 |
| United Utilities Group | Water | 12.8 | 15.1 | |
| TUI Travel | Travel & Tourism | 12.7 | 9.4 | 0.7 |
| Morrison (Wm) Supermarkets | Food Retailers & Wholesalers | 12.7 | 11.7 | 0.8 |
| Kingfisher | Home Improvement Retailers | 12.6 | 12.0 | 0.9 |
| Prudential | Life Insurance | 12.4 | 10.4 | 1.0 |
| Xstrata | General Mining | 12.3 | 8.1 | 0.8 |
| Barclays | Banks | 12.2 | 9.0 | 0.2 |
| Whitbread | Restaurants & Bars | 12.2 | 12.0 | 1.0 |
| Anglo American | General Mining | 12.1 | 8.6 | 1.4 |

| GKN | Auto Parts | 12.0 | 10.1 | 0.7 |
|---|---|---|---|---|
| Investec | Investment Services | 12.0 | 7.8 | 0.2 |
| Sainsbury (J) | Food Retailers & Wholesalers | 11.4 | 11.8 | 1.3 |
| Severn Trent | Water | 11.2 | 14.4 | 1.3 |
| ITV | Broadcasting & Entertainment | 10.9 | 9.0 | 0.6 |
| BT Group | Fixed Line Telecommunications | 10.6 | 9.5 | 1.6 |
| Royal Dutch Shell | Integrated Oil & Gas | 10.5 | 8.3 | 1.5 |
| Scottish & Southern Energy | Conventional Electricity | 10.5 | 13.0 | 1.7 |
| National Grid | Multiutilities | 10.4 | 11.7 | 1.7 |
| Marks & Spencer Group | Broadline Retailers | 10.3 | 10.4 | 1.3 |
| Next | Apparel Retailers | 10.2 | 9.6 | 1.1 |
| Standard Life | Life Insurance | 9.7 | 12.4 | 0.6 |
| Rio Tinto | General Mining | 9.3 | 7.2 | |
| Eurasian Natural Resources Corporation | General Mining | 8.3 | 13.6 | 1.0 |
| Legal & General Group | Life Insurance | 8.3 | 8.2 | 2.0 |
| BAE Systems | Defense | 7.8 | 7.7 | 1.7 |
| Vodafone Group | Mobile Telecommunications | 7.6 | 10.7 | 1.2 |
| Centrica | Gas Distribution | 7.6 | 12.3 | 1.5 |
| AstraZeneca | Pharmaceuticals | 7.6 | 7.5 | |
| Kazakhmys | General Mining | 7.2 | 6.4 | |
| Aviva | Life Insurance | 6.4 | 6.8 | 0.5 |
| Resolution Ltd | Life Insurance | 3.9 | 12.3 | 0.4 |
| International Consolidated Airlines Group SA | Airlines | | 12.3 | 0.3 |
| Capital Shopping Centres Group | Retail REITs | | 21.8 | |
| Cairn Energy | Exploration & Production | | 10.2 | |
| BP | Integrated Oil & Gas | | 6.6 | |

# GLOSSARY

### absolute return funds

A type of investment fund that is designed to provide a positive return in all market conditions. To achieve this objective most use futures, options, derivatives and leveraged investments.

### AIM (Alternative Investment Market)

The London Stock Exchange's market for small companies. It enables companies to obtain a listing at a lower cost and less stringent criteria as is the case for a full quotation.

### asset allocation

Refers to the process of dividing your investment capital between asset classes such as cash, bonds, equities, property and commodities. The balance chosen will have a major impact on the growth and risk of a portfolio.

### bear

A person who thinks the market will fall.

### beta

Measures the sensitivity of the price of a security (e.g. a share) to movements in the market as a whole. If a share has a beta of one, it is expected to move in line with the market; for example, if the market increases by 2%, one would expect the share also to increase 2%. If a share has a beta of two, it would be expected to move twice as much for any given move in the market.

### bid/offer spread

The difference between the quoted selling price (bid price) and the quoted buying price (offer price).

### blue chip stocks

Phrase used to refer to mature companies with strong reputations and perceived to be high quality. The phrase is apparently derived from poker where the highest value chips are blue.

### Bollinger Bands

Lines that are displayed on each side of a moving average line on a share price chart. It runs two standard deviations from the moving average and can be used as an indication of the level of volatility in a security and also an indication when the security could be in an overbought or oversold position.

### bull

A person who thinks the market will rise.

### CFD (Contracts for difference)

Leveraged products that allow you to trade on the price movements of stocks, indices, sectors, commodities and currencies. They are high risk products designed for short-term trading.

### chartist

An alternative name for a technical analyst. A person who uses charts of past price behaviour to help forecast future price movements and trends.

### contrarian investing

A method of investing prevailing against the consensus view. Practitioners seek out overbought or oversold shares. Warren Buffett is perhaps the world's most famous contrarian: "Look upon market fluctuations as your friend not your enemy".

## collective investment

An arrangement that allows a number of different investors to pool their money and achieve diversification in a fund that is normally professionally managed. Includes unit trusts, OEICs and investment trusts.

## corporate bonds

Listed debt issued by companies and quoted daily on the markets, which have a fixed rate of interest and a specific repayment date that can be up to 30 years in the future.

## cum

Means "with". Can be applied to various terms such as dividend or rights that indicate the shares are sold or valued with the dividend or rights passing to the purchaser. Opposite of "ex".

## derivatives

Generic name for financial products whose pricing is derived from other financial products. Examples are CFDs or options.

## dividends

Payment of a portion of the company's post-tax profits to its shareholders. Part of the company's profit is normally retained for reinvestment in future expansion by the company, but the balance is often paid to the shareholders. Often paid in two instalments: interim and final.

## dividend yield

The dividend paid to shareholders expressed as a percentage of the current share price.

## distance to the market

Term used to refer to the difference between the current market price and the condition level of a stop or trailing stop order.

## EPS (earnings per share)

The net profit after taxation and preference dividends have been paid divided by the number of ordinary shares currently issued.

## equities

An alternative name for ordinary shares.

## ETC (exchange traded commodity)

An investment vehicle that tracks the performance of a single or basket of commodities.

## ETF (exchange traded fund)

An investment vehicle that is designed to track the performance of an index or sector. They provide the diversity of a fund, but will trade like a share.

## ex

Means "without". Opposite of "cum". Used as prefix to words such as dividend or rights and indicates that the deal transacted or price quoted is valued without the next dividend or rights issue that would remain with the vendor.

## FST (financial spread trade)

Alternative name for spread betting. A leveraged vehicle similar to CFDs.

## GARP (Growth At a Reasonable Price)

A theory put forward by American investor Peter Lynch. Based on the concept that when a share price stands at fair value the PE of the share will equal its growth rate. The application of this theory means that a fairly priced share will have a PEG of one, and a PEG of less than one would indicate a share is undervalued at the current price.

## Gearing

This term has two main applications.

It can refer to a feature of derivatives, such as futures or CFDs, where because only a small deposit is required to open a position, the profit/loss on the position magnifies the movement of the underlying asset.

This term can also refer to the level of a company-debts, expressed as a percentage of its equity capital. So a company with a gearing ratio of 60% has a level of borrowing equivalent to 60% of its equity capital.

## gilts

Debt securities issued by the UK government. A conventional gilt offers investors a fixed annual interest and a guarantee of repayment at par (100p) at a specific date in the future. Gilts are traded on the stock market throughout their term. Their prices will vary mainly in line with interest rate expectations.

The equivalent in the US is a Treasury stock. US treasuries, and sometimes UK gilts, that have less than one year to maturity are very often referred to as T-Bills.

## high low format

On a price chart this type of line not only shows the movement of the price over time but will also display the price range each day.

## indexed linked gilt

These differ from conventional gilts because the interest payments and the capital are adjusted in line with the RPI. This means that both the interest and the principal on redemption paid by these gilts are, in effect, inflation-adjusted.

## investment trust

A collective investment found in the UK. It is a quoted public limited company that invests in other quoted PLCs.

### IPO (initial public offering)

An offering of shares in the equity of a company to the public for the first time. Also called a *flotation*.

### ISA (individual savings account)

A personal tax shelter available to UK residents that is free of all personal taxes. Investors can use this on an annual basis to build up significant funds that they don't have to disclose on their UK tax returns. If you opt for the investment ISA, as opposed to the cash variety, you can use it in effect as a tax-free share dealing account. Although the annual contribution is limited, there is no limit to the value it can grow to. A few investors have even achieved ISA millionaire status.

### kitchen sinking

A company taking an opportunity to announce all the bad news at the same time. This may be when a new chief executive is appointed or when an external crisis can be used as an excuse for previous poor performance.

### leverage

An American term for *gearing*.

### LSE

London Stock Exchange.

### limit order

A price conditional stock market order to buy or to sell. It will state the minimum price at which you are willing to sell, or the maximum price at which you will buy.

### large cap

Abbreviation for large capitalisation. Often refers to the group of largest companies on the stock market as measured by their market capitalisation.

## maiden dividend

The first dividend ever paid by a company.

## market capitalisation

The value of a company calculated by multiplying the current share price by the total number of shares in issue.

## mid cap (capitilisation)

Medium-sized companies measured by the market capitalisation.

## moving averages

A charting tool that allows you to identify price trends. Basically, a smoothed version of a price line taking an average of previous prices over various periods normally ranging from periods of nine days to as long as 200 days.

## NASDAQ

An acronym for the National Association of Securities Dealer's Automated Quotation, the second largest stock exchange in the US, mainly associated with high-tech companies.

## NIKKEI

Index of the largest 225 companies quoted on the Tokyo Stock Exchange.

## NYSE

New York Stock Exchange.

## overweight

A broker rating for a strong hold, or weak buy (whichever way you want to look at it). The spectrum of brokers' ratings may move from a strong buy, to buy, to overweight, to hold, to underweight and then finally to sell. The term comes from the concept of a market weighting. If, for instance, the pharmaceuticals sector represented 10% of a market by value and an investor had 15% of their portfolio in the pharmaceutical sector, then he would be overweight in pharmaceuticals.

## OEICS (open-ended investment companies)

A type of open-ended collective investment. They are very similar to unit trusts as they are professionally-managed investment funds that provide the investor diversification and access to markets that may be difficult to access in other ways. Some people refer to them as unit trusts in disguise, as they were introduced at the time unit trusts were being criticised on cost grounds. There are differences between unit trusts and OEICs, but they are largely cosmetic.

## PE (price earnings ratio)

The share price of a company divided by the earnings per share. This is one of the most important value-focused stock ratios.

## PEG

The PE divided by the forecast annual growth in earnings per share.

## PIBS (permanent interest bearing shares)

Bonds issued by building societies that provide a fixed interest return and are quoted on the LSE; as such the price and therefore yield will constantly vary on the markets. PIBs issued by building societies that have since been demutualised and become banks are referred to as Perpetual Sub Bonds (PSBs). Both PIBs and PSBs are ranked as subordinated debt and will rank below other classes of debt in the event of a liquidation .

## placing

A method of introducing a new share issue to the market. Unlike an IPO, which is offered to the public, with a placing the company's broker contacts their own clients and offers the shares to them.

## pound cost averaging

Refers to the process of investing by drip-feeding a fixed amount of money into the markets.

## preference shares

A hybrid between an ordinary share and a bond – regarded by many as neither fish nor fowl. They pay a fixed dividend and rank ahead of ordinary shares for dividend payments and also in a company liquidation. However, they do not share in the equity of a company as ordinary shares do. Each issue has different features.

## redemption yield

Sometimes referred to as the *yield to maturity*. It is the return expressed as a percentage if the bond is held to maturity, taking into account not only the annual interest payments but also the capital gain or loss made on maturity.

## resistance

A level on a price chart when previously a rising share price reversed.

## rights issue

A rights issue is a form of corporate action by which a company seeks to raise cash by issuing new shares to current shareholders in proportion to their existing holdings at a price that is normally significantly discounted to the prevailing market price.

## Rule of 20

A dynamic strategic asset allocation strategy. You add the rate of inflation to the forward PE of the equity market: if the aggregate is less than 20, the rule suggests that you increase your equity allocation more than 20, the rule suggests you should reduce it.

### scrip (issue/dividend)

Often referred to as a bonus or capitalisation issue. Shares allocated free to a company's shareholders in proportion to their current holdings. The result is to increase the number of shares in issue and therefore reduce the share price.

A *scrip dividend* is where the investor opts to take shares in lieu of the dividend.

### SETS

Stock Exchange Electronic Trading System. Order-driven electronic trading system used by the LSE for the normal trading of main shares.

### SIPP (self-invested personal pension)

A self-managed pension for UK tax payers in which the investor can not only have a tax-free dealing account but obtain tax relief on capital invested.

### small caps

Companies with low market capitalisations.

### spiked out

A sharp move up or down in a price that triggers stop orders, quickly followed by the price reverting to its original level.

### stop order

An order to buy or sell shares when the share price hits a specified level. For stop buys, the condition level is placed above the prevailing market price; for stop sells, the condition level is placed below the prevailing market price.

### support

On a price chart, a level at which a falling share price previously reversed.

## TER (total expense ratio)

A measure of the total cost for the management or administration of an investment fund such as an ETF or unit trust. Normally expressed as a percentage.

## trailing stop order

A dynamic order to buy/sell shares when the share price rises from its lowest price/falls from its future peak price by a specified number of pence.

## unit trusts

An open-ended collective managed investment fund.

## x-dividend (ex-dividend)

A status achieved by a share when the next dividend will be retained by the present owner even if the share is sold prior to the payment date. Normally, a share goes "XD" about six weeks prior to the dividend payment date.

## yield to maturity

See redemption yield.

# INDEX

Printed in Great Britain
by Amazon.co.uk, Ltd.,
Marston Gate.